Decoding Mammon

Decoding Mammon

Money as a Dangerous and Subversive Instrument

Peter Dominy

WIPF & STOCK · Eugene, Oregon

DECODING MAMMON
Money as a Dangerous and Subversive Instrument

Wipf & Stock
An Imprint of Wipf and Stock Publishers
199 W. 8th Ave., Suite 3
Eugene, OR 97401
www.wipfandstock.com

ISBN 13: 978-1-60608-535-6
Manufactured in the U.S.A.

This book is a condensed version of the author's PhD thesis for the University of Exeter, approved in 2011, entitled "De-Coding Mammon: Money in Need of Redemption," which is available on the university Web site at http://hdl.handle.net/10036/3065, and to which readers are referred for a more detailed treatment of the subject.

Contents

Foreword

by Canon Peter Challen
Chair of the Christian Council for Monetary Justice (UK)

IT IS WITH DEEP relief that I recommend this manageable study of the place money has taken in the human psyche, mind, and economy. It is manageable, while still making reference to many of the most important studies of and observations on the matter of money across many centuries, and pointing to its bearing so ominously on our societal problems today. It brought immediately to mind a sentence that has haunted me throughout the current world crisis of confidence: "A contradiction lies at the heart of the great sadness of our civilization that by using money we turn the world into it."

Since 2008 those concerned to examine, on the basis of escalating evidence of things going awry, and somehow to change the dominant money/credit system in the Western economy, have been "overwhelmed with insurmountable opportunities," to quote Charlie Brown, that "main street" philosopher. Many assume there will be incremental changes on the return to societal sanity, others believe deep-rooted changes in both human minds and in economic structures are required. But, in my understanding, these can and must work together, as a palliative to anguish, but also as a cure to the embedded and erroneous destructiveness of the system itself.

The arrival of this book, born of a toughly tested PhD thesis, for which hard, persistent research was undertaken over seven years, comes as a huge aid to the advance of inclusive justice. Let me explain.

An interdisciplinary study published in 1962 by a church-initiated commission in Scotland concluded that the monetary system is fraudulent. It received scant attention. The market economy was vibrant and it was assumed that its benefits would surely filter down throughout the system.

But a small human force to challenge and to seek for change was generated, which became the Christian Council for Monetary Justice (CCMJ). Its aspiration was to awaken people, secular agencies, and churches to the insidious evil of a system of money creation and distribution that relentlessly increased the rich/poor divisions of society at an exponential rate. The CCMJ focused its case around the compounding of interest beyond justifiable transaction fees, embedded in money creation by commercial banks, which ancient presentations of political economy—upheld by all the major religious traditions—spoke of with such suspicion. But that was just one aspect of the hold money was having over culture in its entirety, which this study shows to be so dangerous and subversive.

The CCMJ, led by laity, ignored by most ordained clergy, made little headway over fifty years against conscious and unconscious vested interests, in church, city, or among the public in general—those for whom the developing financial system brought remarkable material benefit or an unthinking belief that sooner or later it would. Many were the remonstrations within and beyond church membership about morals and values, yet few serious attempts to define structures perpetuating exploitative gains for a few at extended expense of the many.

The emphasis on personal salvation in an individualized society has led to the neglect of an enduring message—that the church is custodian of mutually just relationships and guidelines for conducting trade that are expressions of a universal vision of love.

Now this deep and wide survey of the relevant argument in the Christian tradition is to hand. It serves to introduce a huge range of profound reflection on and deciphering of the intricate complexity of the long-evolving way money has turned matters of intrinsic worth in a fairly trading society into an unfathomable range of commodities with blind powers of exploitation.

We learn within it that neoliberal capitalism is premised on a materialist value system that penetrates the entirety of human life, commodifying everything from human life to the natural world in the service of maximizing a "good" defined largely in terms of material consumption. Yet this ethical system is responsible not only for the escalation of multiple global crises, but simultaneously for high levels of psychological illness and distress around the world. It is therefore a value system divorced from reality, at odds with human nature and with the natural world.

This book shows how this state is deplored in the vision of the kingdom of God—focused on right relationships with the planet and between all its people. *Decoding Mammon* reminds us that there is more about money and justice in the Bible than any other matter that touches all aspects of our daily lives. Unconditional love is the premise; the outcome, structures that are fair to all.

Acknowledgments

THIS BOOK IS INSPIRED by all those who campaign and labor night and day for the sake of the victims of economic systems in which money has proved to be a dangerous and subversive instrument. It is hoped that the material provided here will give them a new understanding of the battle in which they are involved and fresh enthusiasm to continue.

In the seven years of research that the book summarizes, I am particularly indebted to Professor Tim Gorringe of Exeter University for his patience over such a long period, and for all the invaluable advice he has given.

I am also deeply indebted to my wife, Janet, and to all my family and friends for their unfailing support, and for their willingness to forego my participation in activities in which they might otherwise have expected my involvement during the first years of retirement. I trust that the result will prove it has been worth the cost.

Introduction

OF COURSE, THE SUBTITLE of this book is deliberately provocative. The reader will know that the almost universal conviction about money is that it is a positive or neutral instrument. Those who turn to the Bible for inspiration tend to quote 1 Timothy 6:10, where it is asserted (at least, in the Authorized Version and the Revised Standard Version) that it is the *love* of money that is the root of all evil, rather than money in itself. This understanding needs to be tempered first, however, by a recognition that those translations are not the most favored in recent years. In the Good News Bible (1966), the New International Version (1973), and the New Revised Standard Version (1989), the love of money is "a root (or source) of all kinds of evil"—in other words, not the only root, and not of all evil. In fact, this book is not written to deny what St. Paul may have said. The writer is as convinced as anyone that the love of money is a root of all kinds of evil. What this book intends to demonstrate, however, is that it is not sufficient to lay so much of the blame for our troubles on the *love* of money. What is to be maintained is that money *in itself* is equally to blame.

To be more precise, the purpose of this book is to demonstrate the negative view of money that is revealed in the long-term Christian tradition, from the book of Genesis to the present day, and is implied in the famous statement of Jesus, "You cannot serve God and Mammon." This stands in contrast to the general view of economists, politicians, theologians, and the general public, that a person can use it wisely or unwisely, but that there is nothing wrong with money in itself. It is also in stark contrast to the prevailing philosophy of neoliberalism, which advocates the removal of all possible restrictions on the use of money, or "free markets," in the belief that markets work best when money can circulate freely with minimum regulation. In fact, it is my contention that it is this positive or neutral view of money that has produced many of the problems in contemporary society, both in the West and in the rest of the world, that it was central to the optimism that led to the severe financial crisis that surfaced in 2007, and that (unless repudiated) will lead to the comprehensive destruction of the environment.

That is not to say that money is of no use or should be replaced. On the contrary, it is difficult to imagine any advanced society without money, and money has been a major force in the development of the world and the improvement of living standards. My concern is that, in concentrating on the positive effects of the use of money, there has been a tendency to ignore its negative effects. In this respect, we might compare it with fire, which has numerous useful effects, but is still very dangerous, and needs to be treated with great care. And the great difference between fire and money is that money is not created by God, but by selfish human beings, usually those with the greatest power, who have tended to arrange all the rules for its use to suit their own advantage.

It is not my purpose to produce specific remedies for the problems created by money in the present day. In order to avoid the dangers of abstract theorizing, I shall from time to time make suggestions (or refer to the suggestions of others) as to what an economy could be like if money could be redeemed and its negative effects removed. However, this is fundamentally a task for economists and politicians as they face their particular situations. Rather, it is my intention to alert the Christian community to an aspect of its tradition that has been neglected or forgotten, so that those who have the expertise to produce proposals for monetary reform may be able to take account of the theology enshrined in that tradition.

At the same time, I would hope that a better appreciation of the nature of money would help individual Christians and Christian groups to make decisions on the use of their money based on more Christian foundations. Joerg Rieger writes, "What if money were to shape not only our actions and programmatic initiatives, but also our faith and our most cherished images of the divine, without anyone noticing?"[1] The dominant ideologies of each age can have influence at a deep level of consciousness, and there is for all Christians a continual need, in the words of St. Paul, not to "conform any longer to the pattern of this world, but [to] be transformed by the renewing of [their] mind. Then [they] will be able to test and approve what God's will is—his good, pleasing and perfect will" (Romans 12:2).

---

1. Rieger, *No Rising Tide*, 79.

The Word *Mammon*

The word *mammon* occurs only four times in the New Testament: in the AV and RSV versions of Matthew 6:24 and Luke 16:9, 11, 13. It is an Aramaic word that Matthew and Luke made no attempt to translate into Greek, merely transliterating it as *mamonas*. The translators of AV and RSV have also transliterated it for their English versions—though other English versions have opted for translations like "wealth" (NRSV) and "money" (NEB, GNB, NIV).

The derivation of the original Aramaic word is the subject of some debate among scholars. Hauck links it with the verb *'aman*, to mean "that in which one trusts,"[2] while Nestle suggests it might also mean "what is entrusted to man" or "that which supports and nourishes man."[3] In any case, it is clear that *mammon* did not refer only to money. It encompassed property, possessions, wealth, or riches, whatever these might actually consist of.

It is interesting to consider why Matthew and Luke made no attempt to translate the word *mammon* into Greek. It could be because their readers understood what it meant, or because it had become a term in common use in the Christian community. On the other hand, it may have been the difficulty of finding a Greek word that gave an adequate translation. Probably the safest way of rendering it in English would be "mammon," following the same tactic as Matthew and Luke. However, in the conditions of our day, "wealth" or "money" are more readily understood. For myself, I am happier with the broader term "wealth," but acknowledge that how much someone possesses is now described in most societies in monetary terms.

There is also some debate as to whether mammon has a neutral or negative connotation in the words of Jesus. In rabbinic writing, the word was basically neutral, as in the targum to Proverbs 3:5 ("Honor God with your mammon"), the Palestinian Targum to Deuteronomy 6:5 ("You shall love Yahweh your God with . . . all your mammon"), and in the Qumran writings.[4] It was, in fact, a general article of faith among Jews that riches were a sign of God's blessing (e.g., Deuteronomy 28:1–14; Job 42:9–17).

2. Hauck, "Mamonas," 388.

3. Nestle, "Mammon," 2914.

4. For a list of references in the targums, see Schmidt, *Hostility to Wealth in the Synoptic Gospels*, 197.

However, mammon often acquired a negative connotation where wealth had been dishonestly gained or dishonestly used (as, for instance, in bribery; Palestinian Targum 1 Samuel 8:3; 12:3; Isaiah 33:15; Amos 5:12).

On this basis, it can be argued that in everyday usage "mammon" was generally neutral in tone, and this interpretation seems to be supported by Jesus's argument in Luke 16:1–12 in the parable of the "unjust steward," where the master commends the steward for his shrewdness in financial matters. This parable has been the source of much confusion. (How could anybody be commended for doing something so deceitful?) The confusion is much clarified, however, if it is appreciated that loans from a Jew to fellow Jews were condemned in the Mosaic law. J. D. M. Derrett suggests very plausibly that the master could thus have been very grateful to the steward for putting right his transgression.[5] The epithet "unjust" should then be understood as referring to the steward's previous activities for which he was about to be dismissed.

Jesus goes on in this passage to urge his own followers to emulate the shrewdness of the steward by using "unrighteous mammon" (AV) / "worldly wealth" (NIV, NEB, GNB) to gain friends for themselves, so that when it is gone, they will be welcomed into heavenly dwellings (Luke 16:9). Here the encouragement seems to be, not to treat mammon as evil, but to use it honestly—even though it is described as "unrighteous mammon."

The difficulty with this, however, is that "unrighteous" (AV and RSV) and "dishonest" (NRSV) seems to be much more accurate translations of the Greek *adikos* than "worldly," and it could be deduced from this that, despite contemporary usage, Jesus himself regarded mammon as intrinsically evil. The alternative would be to see it as just another example of the way that Jesus often provoked his listeners by exaggerated language. From the rest of his teaching, however, we can see clearly, how Jesus regarded riches as a great spiritual danger to human beings. In Mark 4:19 he talks of "the deceitfulness of wealth." In Mark 10:23–25 he says, "How hard it is for the rich to enter the kingdom of God." And Myers is probably right to see in Jesus's answer to the question about tribute to Caesar a profound skepticism about the money in circulation in his day. Jesus himself did not carry a denarius, nor would any serious Jew, partly because of the

---

5. Derrett, *Law in the New Testament*, 48–77.

emperor's image which it bore, and partly because of its inscription describing Caesar as "august and divine son."[6]

There is in Luke 16:12 an intriguing (apparent) reference to unrighteous mammon as "that which is another man's" (AV), "that which is another's" (RSV), "what belongs to another" (NRSV, NEB), "what belongs to someone else" (GNB), or "someone else's property" (NIV). J. N. Geldenhuys takes this to be a clear indication that Jesus regarded mammon (i.e., everything we possess) as belonging primarily to God, who lends it to us liberally in order that it may be a blessing to us and to others, and that it should be used to honor God.[7] This theme is not stated specifically anywhere else by Jesus, but it does fit in with ideas found in the Old Testament. In Leviticus 25:23, God is recorded as saying explicitly, "the land is mine." In 1 Chronicles 29:11-14, David says, "Everything comes from you, and we have given you only what comes from your hand." Martin Hengel feels that the interpretation of property as a "loan" entrusted by God, which has played so great a role in modern Christian discussion of property, can certainly be found in the preaching of Jesus, but considers it not to be of central significance.[8] Be that as it may, if mammon is a loan from God, this does suggest that mammon was not, in his mind, intrinsically evil. In general terms, however, there can be no doubt that (for reasons that will emerge in this treatment) Jesus's attitude to mammon was one of considerable suspicion.

One further point concerns whether Jesus was giving personality to mammon in his references to it. This is another theme taken up by later writers, famously by John Milton.[9] I asked earlier *why* Matthew and Luke did not try to translate "mammon" into Greek; one reason could be that they felt Jesus was giving it personality. Mammon is certainly regarded by Jesus as a rival to God, but this does not necessarily mean that he regarded it as a person. If he regarded it as a god, that god could be personal or impersonal. St. Paul talks about covetousness (the love of riches?) as "idolatry" (Colossians 3:5; Ephesians 5:5), which could be taken as implying that he regarded money as an idol rather than a god. I shall later

---

6. Myers, *Binding the Strong Man*, 311.

7. Geldenhuys, *Commentary on the Gospel of Luke*, 417.

8. Hengel, *Property and Riches in the Early Church*, 29.

9. Milton, *Paradise Lost*, part one, 579-80, and extensively in part two.

express a preference for regarding money as an instrument created by human beings and turned into a god by human attitudes toward it.

I conclude this section, however, with the key affirmation of Jesus with reference to mammon: "You cannot serve God and mammon." This is stated without any qualification. According to Jesus, anyone "serving" mammon would be serving a rival to God. Obviously, this does not refer to the mere possession or use of mammon, but means that everyone who makes the accumulation and enjoyment of earthly goods the main object of one's life is actually serving mammon rather than God. In the words of W. D. Davies and Dale C. Allison, "God commands an exclusive allegiance and obligation which must transcend all other claimants for a person's soul; while mammon, once it has its hooks in human flesh, will drag it where it wills, all the time whispering into the ear dreams of self-aggrandizement. The marching orders of God and of mammon are in entirely different directions."[10]

In normal human affairs it may be possible to serve two masters. Not so, however, if the relation is that of slavery (as in these passages) or if one of the masters is God—for God demands absolute obedience in every aspect of life. Jesus was speaking here to his disciples, establishing a basic principle about how they were to live in the kingdom he was setting up. This study begins, therefore, with a strong and uncompromising word from the founder of the Christian faith, which was bound to exercise enormous influence throughout the whole history of the Christian church.

10. Davies and Allison, *Commentary on Matthew*, 642.

SECTION ONE

The Nature of Money

Chapter One

What Is Money?

To discover whether money should be regarded as dangerous, we need first to consider what money actually is. When most people think about it, they imagine something simple and straightforward, easily identified and understood. The truth is, however, that money is extremely complex, and as we realize this, we shall be in a position to appreciate both the many problems it creates and the attitudes developed towards it in the Christian tradition.

One of the basic misunderstandings about money is to imagine it as a commodity like other commodities. It is now understood by scholars, however, that the idea of money (as a measure of value) was present in the world long before there was any commodity fulfilling that role.[1] Even in the process of barter it could be said that those involved in the exchange were comparing their products with each other in accordance with some more abstract measure of their respective values. Even before barter exchanges, it can be argued that the idea was present long ago in gifts given to superiors (the size of the gift demonstrating the importance of the person in the community); in peace offerings to people who had been offended (for instance, blood money, offerings to gods, spirits, or ancestors; the size of the offering demonstrating the seriousness of the offence); and in bride money (whether bride-price or dowry). We also find powerful rulers taxing their subjects in different ways—and some of the earliest writing is actually elementary bookkeeping, on clay tablets, recording the amount of taxation paid.[2]

---

1. This point is made continually in Ingham, *Nature of Money*.
2. Davies, *A History of Money*, 11–13 and 23.

The first commodities functioning as money were of various kinds, especially grain and cattle (the wealth of Abraham and Job was measured by the number of cattle they possessed; Genesis 13:2; Job 1:3). One commodity that survived in some places until the mid-twentieth century (AD!) was the cowrie shell. Precious metals came into early use for this purpose, sometimes in the form of ingots or jewelry. The first coinage is traditionally attributed to Croesus, King of Lydia (a Greek kingdom in modern-day Turkey) in about 640–630 BC,[3] and from that time onwards coinage became the dominant form of money. Its great advantage was that it combined a fixed amount of metal with a seal guaranteeing its authenticity.

One of the features of the so-called Dark Ages was that the system based on coinage virtually collapsed, though there remained a skeleton economy based on the Roman accounting system, where debts could be settled in a wide variety of commodities.[4] In Britain the country reverted for about two hundred years to what seemed to be a completely moneyless economy until the people relearned how to mint and use coinage.[5] The money used during that period has sometimes been described as "ghost money" (in existence, but not visible). The amount of coinage began to increase substantially in the tenth century, when there was an agricultural revolution based on developments in agricultural techniques (providing increasing surpluses for sale), a steady increase in population, the development of local markets, a gradual increase in international trade, and a modest development of cottage industries.[6] This led in turn to developments in the area of banking.

In the first instance, bankers were moneychangers who changed money from one currency to another for the purposes of international trading. Then, around the year 1200, they started to take deposits of cash for safe keeping. With the cash deposited with them, these early bankers then made loans to other customers, on which they made various charges. After this came the settling of accounts by bank transfer or bill of exchange (rather than by large crates of cash). The real beginning of banking, however, came when loans started to be made by bank credit,

3. Herodotus, *Histories* 1.29.

4. Ingham, *Nature of Money*, 105.

5. Davies, *A History of Money*, 116.

6. Little, *Religious Poverty and the Profit Economy in Medieval Europe*, 8–15.

which didn't necessarily have to be linked to the cash that banks had deposited with them, provided that all depositors didn't claim their money at the same time. Technically, this is known as fractional reserve banking. Its effect was to create new money "out of nothing." Further changes came through the invention of the printing press, which enabled coins to be printed, and then bank notes—though the first notes were not printed till 1661 by the Bank of Sweden.[7] More immediate in its effects was the far-flung trading of Spain and Portugal and the "voyages of discovery" which took Christopher Columbus to the "new world" in 1492 and Vasco da Gama to India in 1499, followed by many others in the ensuing years. This produced a flood of gold and silver into Europe—which, if properly invested, could have enabled great developments in the European economy. Much of it was spent, unfortunately, on inter-European wars, and the sudden increase in the amount of money in circulation simply led to a great increase in prices (inflation).[8]

The first important public bank (backed by a government or city council) was established in Amsterdam in 1609. This example was followed in Britain in 1694 with the establishment of the Bank of England, to which were given the dual responsibilities of "lender of last resort" (to other British banks) and of control over the issue of currency.[9] This was a creation of tremendous importance to Britain, as it took control of the monetary system out of the hands of the crown and enabled the possibility of creating large sums in loans, backed by the state (which could always cover them by taxation). The loans of the bank were backed by its holdings of gold and silver. Immediately, however, loans were made (particularly to finance government military operations) where such backing was far less than the money lent out. Such lending was acceptable as long as the bank retained public trust, but there was obviously great potential for abuse. In 1844 the Bank Charter Act put a ceiling on note issues by the bank (and other banks). Designed to protect the value of the pound, this provided a degree of stability to the British money system for nearly one hundred years.[10]

7. Chown, *A History of Money from AD 800*, 131.

8. Galbraith, *A History of Economics*, 34–35.

9. Davies, *A History of Money*, 254–62.

10. Ibid., 313.

The history of the capitalist system over the last two hundred years has been one long struggle to keep economies stable in a system that is essentially unstable. Probably the most effective tool has been the Gold Standard formally established by Britain in 1821 and held intact until 1914 and for shorter periods since. The chronic problem of inflation (with its attendant reduction in the value of money) has been tackled in many different ways, particularly by fiscal policy and monetary policy. In the Great Depression of the 1930s, when nothing else seemed to work, J. M. Keynes encouraged governments to create extra money in order to get their economies moving.

After the Second World War, the agreements made at the Bretton Woods conference were an attempt to put the global financial system back on a secure foundation. An initial hope had been that it might be possible set up an international central bank. This was thwarted, however, by the desire of the United States to maintain its economic supremacy—and the result was, instead, the creation of the International Monetary Fund (IMF), funded by contributions from member states, which would seek to maintain economic stability by loans to countries facing difficulties. A major tactic was to maintain fixed exchange rates between currencies in relation to the U.S. dollar (which itself was pinned to gold), the dollar being given in this way equal status with gold as a reserve currency.

Though this system served well for a time, U.S. holdings of gold (compared to dollars) fell steadily, until the United States could no longer hold to the agreed ratio and abandoned it in 1971. In the same way, the IMF was not able to hold to the agreed ratio between its deposits and its loans. To deal with this latter problem, a further reserve asset was created, called "Special Drawing Rights." From 1975 it was recognized that the Deutschmark, the Yen, the Swiss Franc, Sterling, and the French Franc could also be treated as reserve currencies. All these assets have been used by the IMF to bail out currencies in difficulty, but with conditions attached that have often been too hard for a country to bear. Designed to enable countries to repay their debts to the IMF and other international creditors, these conditions have often prevented governments from developing their countries as they might wish, and they have exaggerated the imbalances that they were supposed to correct.

The World Bank, created at the same time as the IMF, was intended originally to make development loans for reconstruction following the Second World War, moving on after that to make loans to any developing country. Here also, however, the conditions attached to loans have often proved too burdensome. One of the great objections to both these institutions is the exaggerated influence of those countries providing most of their capital. A third creation of Bretton Woods was the General Agreement on Trade and Tariffs (known since 1995 as the World Trade Organization), which was formed to agree on common rules for tariffs and to reduce trade restrictions through a series of negotiating rounds. Although some progress has been made in this area, there remains, unfortunately, a reluctance on the part of some of the more powerful nations to abandon practices that are to their benefit.

Further attempts to produce stability have come in the regulations of the Bank for International Settlements (which preceded the IMF, and established an international gold clearing system, balancing credits and debits between countries, in order to minimize actual gold shipments). The first of these (known as Basel I, 1988) required central banks to hold capital equal to ten percent of their risk-weighted assets. Basel II (2004) was more flexible, establishing figures according to a number of relevant factors. Basel III (2010) (agreed to as a result of the recent financial crisis) has raised the required holdings to 9.5 percent in times of crisis. Another attempt to create stability has been the European Monetary Union. In order to enter the Union, member states had to achieve convergence at various levels—fiscal deficits, price stability, exchange rate stability, and interest rates.[11] Continuing membership would require maintenance of these convergences, but the European Central Bank would give assistance in time of crisis. The introduction of the Euro has created a new phenomenon in the form of a currency shared by several countries. Meanwhile, the U.S. dollar has (for all intents and purposes) achieved the status previously held by gold, but remains under U.S. control.

Deregulation

Probably the most significant events of the recent past, however, have been the deregulation of many financial processes encouraged by neo-liberal thinking. This thinking represents a revival of the laissez-faire economics given its classic exposition in the work of Adam Smith. Its

---

11. Treaty Sections 104(c) and 109(1).

best known modern expositors have been Friedrich Hayek[12] and Milton Friedman.[13] Basically, this thinking involves two main theses: (1) that a free-market economy is the best way to economic progress, and (2) that government intervention in the economy should be reduced to a minimum. In the area of national economic policy, this means believing in the removal of all obstacles to free markets, and the minimum of government activity in promoting social welfare. In the area of international policy, it means objecting to all forms of protectionism and encouraging the free movement of both goods and capital. The relevance of these theses to our concerns is that this approach has become the dominant economic philosophy in recent years, shared even by the Labour governments of Tony Blair and Gordon Brown. It has also had a great influence on the international organizations such as the International Monetary Fund and the World Bank—resulting in the so-called Washington Consensus, by which "structural adjustment programmes" have been imposed on nations as a requirement for receiving loans. The chief elements of IMF "advice" in the 1980s and 1990s were concerned with the reduction of taxes and with increasing privatization and market liberalization (all central tenets of neoliberal thinking). In many cases, however, results have not been encouraging, and a strong protest movement has developed, demonstrated particularly by the protest marches around meetings of the IMF and of the G8 nations.

There has also developed a considerable literature critical of the effects of deregulation and the model of a free-market economy. One of the strongest of these critics is John McMurty, who has developed the idea that the philosophy of free markets has become a cancerous invasion of civil and environmental life-organization, in which society's immune system is undermined and disabled, and the sustainability of the external environment threatened.[14] As I shall demonstrate in the next two chapters, it is the freedom to lend without restriction and at any rate of interest that is seen to be at the heart of this invasion, producing what Michael Rowbotham calls in his book title *The Grip of Death*. Joseph Stiglitz (himself a leading official at the World Bank in the 1990s) has written:

---

12. Especially *Road to Serfdom* and *Mirage of Social Justice* (vol. 2 of *Law, Legislation and Liberty*).

13. Especially *Capitalism and Freedom*.

14. McMurty, *The Cancer Stage of Capitalism*.

Not all the downsides of the Washington Consensus policies for the poor could have been foreseen, but by now [2002] they are clear: We have seen how trade liberalization *accompanied by high interest rates* is an almost certain recipe for job destruction and unemployment creation—at the expense of the poor. Financial market liberalization *unaccompanied by an appropriate regulatory structure* is an almost certain recipe for economic instability—and may well lead to higher, not lower, interest rates, making it harder for poor farmers to buy the seeds and fertilizer that can raise them above subsistence. Privatization, *unaccompanied by competition policies and oversight to ensure that monopoly powers are not abused*, can lead to higher, not lower, prices for consumers. Fiscal austerity, *pursued blindly*, in the wrong circumstances, can lead to high unemployment and a shredding of the social contract.[15]

In other words, although Stiglitz is basically a believer in free markets, he has come to realize that allowing money and markets to operate without any restraints does not achieve the desired results.

In recent years, the IMF has changed its emphasis to that of "poverty reduction," and has recognized that too drastic and quick action can be counterproductive. Basically, however, the neoliberal philosophy maintains its dominant position; the same kind of recommendations continue to be made—and protests continue as well.

Contemporary Ramifications

We now encounter a situation in which money exists primarily in the form of bank-created credit—based on the credit-worthiness of the borrower and the confidence inspired by the lender. The ordinary consumer may have a simple bank account, a bank loan, a mortgage, a credit card, a store card, a phone card, and so on. What is not always appreciated is that once a bank has made a loan of any kind, there comes into force a "multiplier effect," whereby the loan (now being treated as part of the total store of money) becomes the basis for further loans. In theory, this process could go on *ad infinitum*, and there are now numerous ways in which credit derivatives have been created. In a situation of "light touch" regulation, the process is only held in check by the risk of banks and other institutions losing their credibility. If they lend too much, banks can get

---

15. Stiglitz, *Globalization and Its Discontents*, 84, my italics.

into serious trouble (like Lehman Brothers in 2008), but governments are very reluctant to see banks go under, for fear of the whole system becoming destabilized. National governments and central banks, similarly, seek to prove the credibility of their currencies, mainly by their efforts to control inflation. Geoffrey Ingham argues (somewhat cynically) that "since the abandonment of monetarist attempts precisely to control the quantities of money in the system, credibility in stable money is assessed in relation to procedural correctness in arriving at interest rates that are intended to regulate the willingness to become indebted."[16] These efforts in themselves are assessed by private credit rating agencies, which have the power to bring down an economy overnight.

Of enormous significance is the rapid increase in the circulation of money brought about by the increasing use of computers for the making of financial transactions (so that billions of pounds or dollars can change hands in a second), the increasing internationalization of economic activity, and the domination of vast multinational corporations, which make it more and more difficult for national governments to exercise control of their economies.

Money as a Commodity

Over the years there has been a persistent belief that money can be treated as a commodity just like other commodities. To this day this remains the opinion of most economists and members of the public. Those who have argued against this belief have usually been sociologists, who have concentrated on the role played by money—so that the medium in which money exists becomes irrelevant. Instead, they maintain that money's particular character is to be found in its role as an abstract measure of value (sometimes called "money of account").[17]

This takes us back to what we said about the beginnings of money— that we can say there was a "money of account" before any commodity was involved. It will be obvious also from what I have described that money as

16. Ingham, *Nature of Money*, 145.

17. The first explicit church support for such an understanding was in 2003 in the report by the Doctrine Commission of the Church of England *Being Human*, which said, "[The word] money is much more like a verb than a noun. . . . What makes notes and coins money is not some quality or intrinsic property they have in themselves, but the function they perform in human society" (Doctrine Commission, *Being Human*, 58).

we know it today bears little resemblance to a commodity. Looking to the future, some writers have written about such ideas as the deterritorialization or denationalization of money, "electronic money," "virtual money," and "the end of money." So, for instance, Friedrich Hayek urged, back in 1976, that government monopolies on the creation of money should be abolished and be replaced by free competition between private banks.[18] Mervyn King (when deputy director of the Bank of England), considering the future of central banks and their creation of money, posited the possibility, as a result of technological innovations, that settlements could be carried out by electronic means without any need to clear through a central bank. In this situation, assets, goods, and services would be priced in terms of a unit of account that could be universal in scope.[19]

What is clear, in hindsight, is that the development of such ideas has been fuelled by developments in the world economy that have made it increasingly difficult to hold to a commodity theory. Fundamental to all has been the ability of public and private banks to produce money by means of loans to their customers, which have increased the stock of money without any necessary connection with silver or gold or anything else in the "real" economy. For many years there was an assumption (or a requirement) that such loans had to have some relation to gold or silver stocks. The fragility of this system was demonstrated, however, in the Great Depression of the thirties, and the situation was ultimately saved only by following the ideas of Keynes that governments should spend their way out of depressions, even if this meant an increase in their public debt. This was tantamount to the abandonment of any commodity theory. Similarly, in the recent economic crisis, the chief solution followed by governments has been to increase dramatically the amount of money in existence through an immense extension of credit. This may have staved off the immediate crisis, but many fear that it may only prolong the life of a flawed and unstable system, and could lead to even worse crises in the years to come. It has certainly made it abundantly clear that money is not a commodity like any other commodity we might know.

The conclusion to this whole discussion must be simply to reemphasize that money is by no means a simple concept, and that it is quite inadequate to regard it as a commodity like other commodities. Instead, it

18. Hayek, *Denationalization of Money*.

19. King, "Challenges for Monetary Policy," 410–11. This argument is taken further by Greco in *The End of Money and the Future of Civilization*, ch. 17.

is whatever anyone is prepared to recognize as money, and most of it has its beginnings in bank-created debt. We are now in a position, therefore, to consider how this problematic nature of money can lead to all sorts of dangers.

SECTION TWO

Lending and Borrowing

CHAPTER TWO

Money and Debt

CREDIT AND DEBT ARE two sides of the same coin. If you concentrate on credit, it is easy to appreciate the advantages of getting access to more money than you happen to possess. In particular, it is possible to argue that credit performs a major role in allowing businesses to access capital for the development of their products before they are able to market them. From this point of view, money has been a key instrument in the enormous development of the world over the last five hundred years.

If you look at the other side of the coin, however, it is possible to get a much more negative picture. Money borrowed has to be paid back. Indeed this is an essential requirement of virtually all economies, certainly of capitalist economies. Otherwise it would have been given as a gift. The problem is that individuals (or companies or governments) are not always able to pay back. Being in debt can then become a distinctly negative experience. For individuals, it may involve carrying for many years a burden that they cannot remove. It could involve losing their house or their land or even their freedom to their creditor—or being declared bankrupt. If large numbers of people find themselves in this position, a whole sector of society could feel alienated from the rest. If a government gets itself into this position, their whole country will suffer.

In fact, right from the beginnings of money, debt has been a recurrent problem, and there are records of situations all the way back to 2400 BC where rulers had to resort to mass cancellations of debt because of the social suffering it was causing.[1] In our own day, debt has become an almost universal experience, as living on credit has come to be accepted as the norm (in contrast to the situation not long ago when you only bought

---

1. Hudson, *The Lost Tradition of Debt Cancellations.*

things with money you had saved). For the most part, people eventually pay their debts, but, unfortunately, there are numerous cases where changed circumstances make repayment difficult (or even impossible) and produce the kinds of suffering we have just mentioned.

While debt cancellations were crisis decisions in other countries, in Israel they were supposed to be part of the regular pattern of life, in that, according to the Mosaic law, any debts not repaid after seven years were to be cancelled (Deuteronomy 15:1–6). This was one aspect of a whole raft of measures aimed at protecting the most vulnerable members of society and ensuring that everyone was able to enjoy (at least) the necessities of life. The ideal was of each person sitting under one's own vine and under one's own fig tree (Micah 4:4). This was not, of course, to deny the value of lending. In fact, lending to the poor was highly commended (Deuteronomy 15:7–9; Psalm 37:26; 112:5) as one way of helping them through difficult circumstances. And, in normal circumstances, it was expected that such debts would be repaid. What the law was recognizing, in this seven-year cancellation of debts, was that, unless unrepayable debts were remitted, some of their people might endure considerable suffering. For the Israelites, this was a religious matter—their God was one who cared for the weak and suffering, and expected his people to do the same.

The only records in the Old Testament of a widespread cancellation of debts are in Jeremiah 34 (where Israelite slaves—made slaves, presumably, because of their debts—were ordered to be released) and in Nehemiah 5:1–13. It is a regular complaint of the prophets, however, that the rich were ill-treating the poor. Buying the poor with silver and the needy for a pair of sandals (Amos 2:6; 8:6) almost certainly refers to making slaves of those unable to pay their debts. In the parable of the Unmerciful Servant (Matthew 18:21–35) and the teaching that precedes it, Jesus made it abundantly clear that his followers were to forgive the debts of those unable to repay them. St. Paul wrote, "Let no debt remain outstanding except the continuing debt to love one another" (Romans 13:8).

As the centuries went by, it seems that the requirement to repay debts began to take precedence over any debt remission. A step in the right direction came with the possibility of suing for bankruptcy. This became possible in Britain in 1571. In the first instance, however, it only applied to traders and craftsmen. Others who couldn't pay their debts were still liable to prison sentences (as we know from the novels of Dickens). This was remedied in 1871 when it became possible for anyone who was insolvent to sue for bankruptcy. Unfortunately, right up to this day, no bankruptcy procedure has been produced for governments.

The catalyst for recent thinking about debt has undoubtedly been the colossal increase in debt in the last thirty years, as numerous regulations have been relaxed (or removed) on the creation of credit. Debt has now become a serious problem for many people. What has most caught the headlines, however, has been the plight of the poorer countries of the world, who have been the recipients of loans that they have not been able to repay. The most dramatic description of their dilemma is that given by Michael Rowbotham in his book *The Grip of Death* (1998), where he says of much of the credit that had been extended to poor countries, "Directed against vulnerable people and executed under the banner of 'aid,' it is an injustice so profound and total and shameful that is quite without parallel in the history of human affairs."[2] Concern about the situation has spread across a wide intellectual and religious spectrum, but it is Christian thinkers and activists who are very often in the fore. Notable amongst these is Ann Pettifor, the chief architect of the Jubilee 2000 movement for the cancellation of the debts of the world's poorest countries, who clearly finds her inspiration in her Christian faith. The result of this campaign was a considerable reduction in the debt of the most heavily indebted countries. In some cases reductions were made in return for improvements in a country's economic structure and policies. In the case of Poland, there was a massive reduction of 50 percent in her external debt. It has to be said, however, that, despite the success of this campaign (and the 2005 Make Poverty History campaign), much remains to be done, and situations remain (for example) where a country's repayments of international debt exceed the cost of all expenditure on health and education, and necessitate drastic reductions in it.

Probably the most significant theological book on the subject is *Grace and Mortgage* (1997) by Peter Selby (then Bishop of Worcester), in which he draws a clear distinction between what he calls an "economy of grace" and an "economy of exchange," suggesting that the Christian church, if it is true to its tradition, should be encouraging economic relations based on generosity (grace) rather than those based on credit and debt (mortgage). In our present culture, he says, credit is rarely extended out of compassion, in order to help someone through a difficult period,

2. Rowbotham, *Grip of Death*, 148.

but simply with the purpose of making profit. He says, "Lending and borrowing can, when the transaction is carried on by two voluntary and equal participants, facilitate the best use of available resources; but it can only do that if its highly dangerous capacity to bind the future and impose the will of the creditor on the debtor are recognised and controlled."[3] His argument is based explicitly on the Old Testament law of debt cancellation—but, even more, on the character of God. And he quotes the famous words of Portia in *The Merchant of Venice*:

> [Mercy] is an attribute of God himself;
> And earthly power doth then show likest God's
> When mercy seasons justice.[4]

Another valuable critique comes from Kathryn Tanner, who, in *Economy of Grace* (2005), suggests that there are many issues where Christians and others could find common cause if they were able to enter into dialogue.[5] To this day, however, the cancellation of debt is still a matter that arouses controversy. Debt repayment has always been important for giving security to lenders. If some debts can be remitted (it is argued), the fundamental requirement of repayment has been undermined, the flow of loans could dry up, and debtors would lose a major source of motivation for putting their house in order. Credit/debt has actually become the foundation of the capitalist system, and it is argued that it is essential if economies are to grow. The Christian answer to this would be that there can be no argument with credit and debt in themselves. In the Mosaic law loans to the poor were encouraged and repayment expected. What that law could be encouraging is simple realism—that repayment will not always be possible, and, in that situation, the most realistic solution is cancellation. On the other hand, as has already been suggested, debt can become a matter of life and death, so a more likely answer could be that the law was intended to protect people from the dangers it can bring.

Credit/debt can be very useful, but the question seems to be, how far should it be allowed to go? And this has been brought to the attention of the whole world by the economic crisis that surfaced in 2007, where the chief perception has been that the crisis was caused by an expansion of credit/debt far in excess of what the system could contain. So the

3. Selby, *Grace and Mortgage*, 68–69.

4. Shakespeare, *The Merchant of Venice*, act 4, scene 1, lines 195–97.

5. K. Tanner, *Economy of Grace*, 89.

Archbishop of Canterbury, for instance, wrote in *The Spectator* that the crisis had exposed "the element of basic unreality in the situation—the truth that almost unimaginable wealth has been generated by equally unimaginable levels of fiction, paper transactions with no concrete outcome beyond profit for traders."[6] From this point of view, the implication of the Mosaic legislation for today is that debt must have its limits. In principle, lending is useful. But at the same time, there are limits—one of which is the ability of debtors to repay.

There remains also a serious doubt as to whether economic growth is as important as some people seem to think. As we shall see later, much of the production in the modern world is of items that nobody needs— rather it is driven by the need to make money in order to repay debts and interest. And one of the most disconcerting effects of this is the unnecessary consumption of the earth's resources and the exacerbation of global warming. Several writers are now researching how it would be possible to have a viable economy that is not based on the imperative of growth. So Tim Jackson, for instance, argues that we need (1) a new growth engine based on nonpolluting energy sources, selling nonmaterial services, not polluting products; (2) a move from an emphasis on consumption to one of ecological investment; (3) a change in human expectations.[7] A more radical proposal advocated by several writers is that all new money released into the economy should be debt free. In *The Ecology of Money* (1999), Richard Douthwaite proposes the issue to each country (according to the size of its population) of international currency consisting of energy-backed currency units (ebcus), and a national issue of currency to be used only for exchange purposes.[8] Thomas Greco holds that the issue of credit/money should be taken out of the hands of governments (and banks) altogether, and be issued free of debt by community credit-clearing agencies.[9]

There is much discussion at the moment (2012) about the structure of the world economy. From Christian theology a strong warning emerges about the dangers of debt, which could require a total reconfiguration of the economy. At the very least, it calls for questions to be asked at

6. Williams, in *The Spectator*, 26 September 2008.

7. T. Jackson, *Prosperity Without Growth*, chs. 8 and 9.

8. Douthwaite, *The Ecology of Money*, 58 and 61–62.

9. Greco, *The End of Money and the Future of Civilization*, 92–98.

many levels, so that the worst effects of debt are tackled and some stability brought to a system that (because of debt) is otherwise fundamentally unstable.

Since borrowing is almost always borrowing at interest, I will now consider the further problems created by interest.

Chapter Three

Money and Interest

THE PRACTICE OF LENDING at interest is now so firmly embedded in our economic system and so accepted as a normal aspect of life that any suggestion to abolish it, or even control it, can be seen as antiquarian, anti-business, and restrictive of human progress. This would be the opinion of most Christians today. The purpose of this chapter is to examine why lending at interest was opposed for so long by Christian writers, and why this opposition could still be relevant today. The earlier literature normally used the word *usury* to refer to any lending at interest, and the early opposition was, therefore, to any lending at interest. More recently, the word has come to refer to lending at excessive rates of interest. However, most of this discussion will be centered on lending at any rate of interest.

The Old Testament Prohibition

We saw in the last chapter that the Jewish law encouraged the giving of loans, even if it required that in certain circumstances they should be cancelled. What was forbidden was the charging of interest. This prohibition is stated three times in the Law (Exodus 22:25; Leviticus 25:35–37; Deuteronomy 23:19–20), the first two referring to loans to the poor, the third to loans to fellow Jews. The difference between the first two and the third has caused much discussion over the years. It has been suggested, for instance, that the third must also refer to loans to the poor. On the other hand, taking the Deuteronomic reference as it stands suggests that it could apply to all loans to fellow Jews, rich or poor. In this case, it might refer not just to charity loans but to commercial loans as well. The matter is further complicated by the particular mention in Deuteronomy that it *would* be possible to take interest from non-Jews, a distinction given particular attention by John Calvin. The distinction may be partly explained by the fact that the Hebrew word used here for a non-Jew is *nokri*, which referred to a temporary resident, who did not have the protection given to the *ger*, a permanent resident who had probably accepted the Jewish faith.

Among the Jewish people it seems that the prohibition was taken to apply to all loans (as, for instance, in Psalm 15:5 and Ezekiel 18:13). The rabbis certainly made no distinctions. The early church Fathers were strongly opposed to taking interest from the poor. Jerome and Ambrose explicitly condemned all taking of interest—except that Ambrose allowed it to be taken from those who could be regarded as enemies (as he understood the provision of Deuteronomy 23:20).

In the teaching of Jesus we find that he only refers to interest in the parables of the Talents and the Pounds, where he seems to accept the payment of interest as part of normal life. However, in Matthew 5:17, he said that he had not come to destroy the Law, but to fulfill it, and that "not the smallest letter, not the least stroke of a pen, will by any means disappear from the Law until everything is accomplished" (Matthew 5:18 niv). On the basis of this passage, therefore, and his frequent quotations from the Law (not to mention the fact that the early church continued to oppose the payment of all interest), we may safely assume that he would have accepted the proscription of interest without question. As far as the parables of the Talents and the Pounds are concerned, where a servant is told that he could have put his master's money on deposit with bankers so that when the master returned he could receive it back with interest (Matthew 25:27 and Luke 19:23), it should be appreciated that this is an incidental part of these stories, the main purpose of which is to teach that Jesus's disciples should be active, using the gifts that God has given them, and it would be very dangerous to draw from so small a detail a doctrine that Jesus never taught elsewhere and would have been in contradiction to the teaching that we find both in the Law and in the early church. If we want explicit teaching of Jesus, we can turn to Luke 6:35, where he encouraged his followers to give generously, even to their enemies, "without expecting anything back" (niv). Though there is no explicit mention here of interest, the spirit Jesus is encouraging would hardly restrict itself to the returning of capital while still requiring the payment of interest.

The Scholastics

Interest was accepted in Roman law, but continued to be opposed by the church, and excessive interest has been opposed by the Roman Catholic Church until the present day. It became a major point of controversy, however, as trade revived in the late Middle Ages, and was much discussed in the revival of learning associated with the scholastics. In general terms, we can say that all the scholastics opposed the charging of interest, but there were many different opinions about the exceptions that might be made. So, for instance, in the writings of Thomas Aquinas (ca. 1225–1274), we have arguments based primarily on the teaching of Aristotle and the idea of natural law, as a result of which Aquinas regarded usury as a sin against justice in exchange, a violation of the requirement of equality of value in everything that was exchanged. He laid much store by Aristotle's opinion that money was invented chiefly for purposes of exchange, concluding that "it is by its very nature unlawful to take payment for the use of money lent."[1]

The principal exceptions allowed by some of the scholastics were *damnum emergens* (where the lender suffered damage or loss through his lending) and *lucrum cessans* (where the lender failed to gain the profit he might have made if he hadn't made the loan). Aquinas says concerning *damnun emergens* that "a lender may without sin enter an agreement with the borrower for the loss he incurs of something he ought to have [e.g., if there is delay in returning a loan]." On the other hand, concerning *lucrum cessans*, he says, "but the lender cannot enter an agreement [at the time of the loan] for compensation, through the fact that he makes no profit out of the money; because he must not sell that which he has not yet."[2] In the case of *damnum emergens*, Aquinas is suggesting that there would be no question of the money itself breeding more money—rather that the money (lent but not returned) could have been used for another purpose. In the case of *lucrum cessans* the money concerned would have been used for the two different purposes of exchange and profit making.[3] Aquinas

1. *Summa Theologica*, q. 78, art. 1, p. 331.

2. Ibid., q. 78, art. 2, p. 335.

3. It should be noted that, in *De Malo*, Aquinas was less accepting of *damnus emergens*. There his argument is that "some say that homes and horses, unlike money, suffer deterioration through use, and so lenders can receive something as compensation for this. But this is no argument, since one accordingly could not justly receive greater compensation for a rented house than the house would thereby lose value. Therefore

was quite happy for interest to be paid where a person puts money into a partnership (as opposed to a loan), on the grounds that the ownership of the money is not transferred to someone else, but remains his own, and risk is shared. The profits made by the partnership can then be attributed to the labor contributed in the partnership rather than to any quality inherent in the money itself.

On the question of the Deuteronomic exception (that interest could be charged to foreigners), Aquinas claimed that this exception no longer applied, since the gospel calls us to treat everyone as our neighbor. The exception in the time of Moses was simply to avoid avarice leading them into the greater evil of taking interest from fellow Jews.[4]

The controversy over usury was to continue for many more years (and in various ways till the twentieth century). The practice that proved most difficult to combat in the fifteenth century was that of the compulsory loans required from citizens by various state governments, on which interest was paid. These loans obviously took the place of taxation, the pill being sugared by the payment of interest. As we shall see, the church developed similar funds for charitable purposes (known as *montes pietatis*), without the payment of interest—but pressure mounted for the covering of expenses.[5] Controversy continued also on the question of bills of exchange—which were agreements to discharge a debt somewhere abroad, at a future date, and in a foreign currency. These were immensely popular, obviating the necessity of transferring large amounts of bullion from country to country, and a great facilitator of trade, being a combination of a credit and an exchange transaction that invariably included the payment of interest.

The matter of interest was finally resolved (if that is the correct word) by Pope Leo X at the Fifth Lateran Council in 1515 through his bull in relation to *Montes Pietatis* (public funds for lending money to the poor), when he allowed interest to be paid from the beginning of a loan in order to cover expenses and indemnify the lender against loss. He continued to define usury as occurring "when, from its use, a thing which produces nothing is applied to the acquiring of gain or profit without any work,

---

we should say that it is licit to sell the use of a home, but not of money" (*De Malo* q. 13, art. 4, reply 4). Nevertheless—possibly because the *Summa* was published later—it is the estimation included in the *Summa* that came to be widely accepted by later scholars.

4. *Summa Theologica*, q. 78, art. 1, pp. 331–32.

5. Noonan, *Scholastic Analysis of Usury*, 295.

any expense or any risk,"[6] but, in his ruling on *Montes Pietatis,* Pope Leo undermined most of the foundations of the church's usury doctrine. By suggesting that interest *could* be paid, provided that it involved labor, cost, or risk, he was sanctioning the main reasons given for charging interest. All that remained was condemnation of the totally idle lender making effortless profit at no risk—together with condemnation of those making inordinate profit (which is the way usury is usually understood today). This seemed to be the end of a long road whereby the activities of both traders and bankers could be justified. Leo stated, "[The public funds] do not introduce any kind of evil or provide any incentive to sin if they receive a moderate sum for their expenses and by way of compensation, provided it is intended to defray the expenses of those employed and other things pertaining to the upkeep of the organizations, and provided that no profit is made therefrom."[7]

John Calvin

The leaders of the Reformation were also conservative in their attitude to usury, but approached it from an entirely different direction. Whereas the scholastics had based their teaching on natural law and had sought to work out precise rules that everybody should follow, the Reformers based theirs on the teaching of the Bible and their conviction that each individual was responsible for applying it in one's own life. In the teaching of Martin Luther are two important points in relation to the question of interest. The first is that he categorically condemned it. The second, however, is that, in his teaching about the "two kingdoms," he handed over to the state the responsibility for formulating and enforcing laws in the secular sphere—so that, however much he and his followers might preach against the taking of interest, there was no guarantee that rulers would follow in the same direction. The same could also be said of John Calvin,[8] except that Calvin was much more sympathetic towards the growing commercial classes and the need for Christians to come to terms with the new economic situation.

---

6. "Fifth Lateran Council," Session 10 (4 May 1515).
7. N. Tanner, *Decrees of the Ecumenical Councils,* 627.
8. Calvin, *Institutes of the Christian Religion,* 4.20.1.

Calvin's doctrine of usury is spelled out in a number of places. In his letter to Claude de Sachins, written in 1543, around the time when this was a burning issue in Geneva, he maintained the strictness of Luther, but was critical of some of the arguments made from Scripture by those opposing the payment of interest. He maintained, for instance, that the word of Jesus in Luke 6:35 ("Lend hoping for nothing in return") "ought to be interpreted that while he would commend loans to the poor without expectation of repayment or the receipt of interest, he did not mean at the same time to forbid loans to the rich with interest." He continued, "It could be wished that all usury and the name itself were first banished from the earth. But *as this cannot be accomplished* (my italics), it should be seen what can be done for the public good." Although he recognized the strength of the biblical opposition to usury, he claimed that "our state today is very different in many respects. Therefore usury is not wholly forbidden among us unless it be repugnant both to justice and to charity."[9]

Calvin succeeded (in his interpretation of the Old Testament texts) in condemning what he regarded as usury (causing harm to the needy) while at the same time making room for equitable commercial transactions. He makes the usury prohibition (a) applicable to loans to the poor, rather than to the rich; (b) applicable to charitable help, rather than to commercial investment; (c) a matter of ethics for God's people, rather than a basis for political law. Such carefully balanced teaching by Calvin may have much to commend it. In fact, it would not be going too far to say that it is the foundation on which most Christian teaching since that time (outside the Roman Catholic Church) has been based. So, for instance, in a report commissioned by the Church Investors Group (of the Church of England) written in 2008, the writers say, "Calvin and others correctly discerned that the main principle behind the Old Testament prohibitions was protection of the poor, a zealous concern that the latter should not be exploited in their vulnerable condition. But they no longer felt that this necessitated a blanket ban on all interest. Effectively, they were exhorting people to live by the spirit of the law rather than the letter of it."[10]

Calvin's teaching differs greatly, of course, from Roman Catholic teaching (which has largely continued the attempt to follow in the tradition of Aquinas and natural law) by his firm rejection of its foundations

9. *Corpus Reformatorum*, vol. 38, part 1, English translation in Beaty and Farley 139–42.

10. Higginson, Parsons, and Clough, *Usury, Investment and the Sub-Prime Sector*, 15.

and by his attempt to apply directly the teaching of the Scriptures. On the other hand, many criticisms can be made of it—not least, that Calvin's treatment of the Scriptures is highly selective.

In the first instance, we take his suggestion that the usury proscription in the Torah was only intended to protect the poor. Leviticus 25:35–36 and Exodus 22:25 are certainly addressed to the particular situation of the poor man who runs into difficulties, and there can be no doubt (as shown earlier) that protection of the poor was a major factor in the determination of Jewish law. In Deuteronomy 23:19, however, the prohibition is not restricted to the poor—nor is it in many later Old Testament references. (And it was not understood in this way by the Fathers of the church.) In fact, it needs greater justification than Calvin gives to say that Deuteronomy 23:19 refers to charitable help, while claiming that the next verse is the basis of a commercial law. As is pointed out by Paul Mills, "If the original author had wished to allow commercial trading for productive purposes, then this distinction could have been used rather than that of brother/foreigner."[11] What is most surprising, perhaps, is Calvin's apparent readiness to disregard an Old Testament law (except for the seventh commandment!) in favor of the "golden rule," when Jesus himself said that "not the smallest letter, not the least stroke of a pen, will by any means disappear from the Law until everything is accomplished" (Matthew 5:18).

Because of its formative influence on future Protestant thinking, Calvin's teaching about usury is still hotly debated today. S. C. Mooney argues, "The modern church owes a great debt to Calvin for his contribution to the bedrock of sound biblical interpretation. . . . However, in matters of economics Calvin failed to distinguish himself."[12] Like other contemporary writers (to whom I shall turn later), Mooney sees the widespread damage that has been done over the ages through the institution of interest, and regards the contribution of Calvin as the turning point. This is, indeed, the assessment of R. H. Tawney, who regards it as a "watershed" in Christian thinking:

> The significant feature in his discussion of the subject is that he assumes credit to be a normal and inevitable incident in the life of society. . . . that acceptance of the realities of commercial practice

11. Mills, "Should Interest Exist?" 30.
12. Mooney, *Usury, Destroyer of Nations*, 162.

> as a starting-point was of momentous importance; it meant that
> Calvinism and its offshoots took their stand on the side of the
> activities which were to be most characteristic of the future, and
> insisted that it was not by renouncing them, but by untiring con-
> centration on the task of using for the glory of God the opportuni-
> ties which they offered, that the Christian life could and must be
> lived.[13]

What this reveals all too clearly is a failure by Calvin to appreciate sufficiently the dangers posed by the use of money. He was certainly aware
of the dangers, as is witnessed by his attempts to control the incidence of
usury. On the other hand, it is significant that he was able to distinguish
two types of usury—one that he considered to be harmful, and one that
was not. So he talked about "biting" usury (which caused harm to the
poor) and legitimate usury (which, provided it didn't harm anyone, could
be used for the benefit of both individuals and society). What he failed to
see, however, was that interest, if it became widespread in society, could
create conditions in which harm could be done to all classes of people—
not least, the poor that he was so keen to protect. In his anxiety to be positive towards the forces that were transforming society, and to reject the
quibbling arguments of the Catholic Church (and the basis on which they
were built), he was persuaded (or deceived?) to turn a blind eye to the
possibility that there might be other ways of ordering an economy—and,
at the same time, to ignore the plain meaning of the scriptural teaching
that he claimed so vociferously to be upholding.

It certainly must have been difficult to see how the institution of
interest, now so well established, could be completely obliterated. It can
even be argued that, whatever Calvin had said, the institution of interest
would have continued to flourish. From the point of view of Christian
theology, however, one can't help feeling that Calvin missed a priceless
opportunity to explore other possible economic systems, based on the
biblical teaching that meant so much to him, and that was supposed to be
the foundation of the totally new theological system advocated in Protes-
tantism. From this point on, it could be said, the die had been cast. In the
words of Benjamin Nelson, "Calvin on Deuteronomy became a Gospel of
the modern era. Everyone from the sixteenth to the nineteenth century
who advocated a more liberal usury law turned to Calvin for support.

---

13. Tawney, *Religion and the Rise of Capitalism*, 116–17.

Even those who would not or could not mention his name were compelled to speak his words."[14]

Since the Reformation

It would be overly simplistic to suggest that, since the Reformation, the Roman Catholic Church has continued in the tradition of Aquinas, and the Protestant churches in the tradition of Calvin. Nevertheless, if we follow through the question of usury, this would be a useful summary. The Roman Catholic Church continued to maintain its opposition to usury, ultimately basing its policy on the encyclical *Vix Pervenit* published by Benedict XIV in 1745, which followed the scholastic denial of usury in general, while allowing extrinsic titles to interest in certain cases. The question of usury was formally settled in 1917 with the issue of the New Code of Canon Law, with the following comprehensive statement:

> If a fungible thing is given someone, and later something of the same kind and amount is to be returned, no profit can be taken on the ground of this contract; but in lending a fungible thing it is not itself illicit to contract for payment of the profit allocated by law, unless it is clear that this is excessive, or even for a higher profit, if a just and adequate title be present.[15]

This is couched in very general terms and has been interpreted in different ways by different writers. What it seems to do, however, is to give freedom of conscience when following the civil law, while, at the same time, maintaining a Catholic moral standard that may often be in conflict with popular opinion.

In the Church of England, disquiet concerning the charging of interest coincided with the rise of the Christendom movement of the early twentieth century, which sought social recovery in the principles of the pre-Reformation church. Some of the most interesting contributions, however, were those of William Temple, who, in his later years, came to appreciate that there would be no lasting solutions to society's problems without a reform of the financial system. Temple's last book, *The Church Looks Forward* (1944), contains a number of addresses given in his final years, including an address to the Bank Officers' Guild in 1943, in which

14. Nelson, *The Idea of Usury*, 74.
15. Roman Catholic Church, *Code of Canon Law*, para. 1735.

he took the opportunity to air a number of his ideas on economic matters. Identifying the two pillars of the Christian economic system in the Middle Ages as the prohibition of usury and the just price, he deduced from the prohibition of usury that "money is in its own nature a medium of exchange, and, therefore, if you use it as a commodity in the sense of trying to profit yourself by variations in its value over against goods, you are destroying it for its proper social purpose; and there are some kinds of activity in this direction which I think public opinion is tending to think ought undoubtedly to be prohibited, as for example, speculation in foreign currencies."[16] In response to a question raised about excessive interest/usury, he responded that the church had always had great difficulty in deciding exactly where the line should be drawn. For himself, he thought that

> the line should probably be drawn between loans for objects that involve some risk, and loans where the principal is really secure and consequently there is no proper partnership in the enterprise; and in the latter case it seems to me that the condemnation of usury requires a limitation upon the return that may be earned. This is quite irrespective of the party making the loan—whether an individual or a bank.[17]

Comment of this kind came to an end with the death of Temple and only revived in the 1990s, as theologians began to come to terms with the effects of deregulation in the world economy. So, in his radical reassessment of the global economy under the title *Capital and the Kingdom*, Timothy Gorringe finally raised again the question of usury:

> The charging of interest, it has been shown, involves a significant transfer of money to the richest groups of a country's population. This systematic transfer of money from those who need it most to those who need it least is one of the factors pushing the world towards catastrophe. It fuels the urge of the very rich, including the huge industrial and financial corporations, to compete with one another purely for the sake of economic wealth and power. It lulls the moderately well off into a complacent sense that all is well with economic life. By artificially increasing the financial pressures on the less well-off and the poor, it deepens their economic dependency. In each of these ways it stimulates an increasingly

16. Temple, *The Church Looks Forward*, 148.
17. Ibid., 59–60.

high level of economic activity and the ecological damage which results. Thus interest is opposed for the very reason it was opposed by the medieval church—because it harms life.[18]

In a later treatment ("Can Bankers be Saved?" [2001]) Gorringe clarifies his thinking by saying he is not necessarily calling for the abolition of usury (unless that means excessive interest). Instead he says, "I will agree with Richard Douthwaite that one could perfectly well recognize a fair or, to use scholastic terminology, a just interest rate which would both reward lenders for the risk they take, compensate for loss of purchasing power, and share the benefit between borrower and lender."[19]

The Problem with Interest

The opinion of most people today, and certainly those most involved in the global financial system, would be that, just as money itself is a basically neutral commodity which has contributed greatly to the development of the world, so interest is an institution that has enabled the sharing of money on a scale that would have been unlikely without it, and has made its own considerable contribution towards the development of the world's resources. In fact, this would probably be the opinion of most Christians—lay people or theologians. In the light of this, one needs to ask why it is that, over the years, Christian writers have expressed so many doubts about it, so that it has taken up far more of their ink than any other aspect of money.

In the first doubts expressed about interest—in the Jewish Torah, taken on (as I have shown) by the prophets, Jesus, the New Testament writers, and the early church Fathers—the chief concern seems to be with those who are unable to pay interest because of their reduced circumstances. This was the same concern as that with the compulsory repayment of debt. Those unable to repay a debt or the interest on a debt were in real danger of having insufficient money or other resources to maintain a reasonable (or even subsistence) standard of living, of losing the land off which they lived, and even of becoming debt-slaves. The conviction behind the Torah, in contrast, was that each person in a community should have sufficient means to maintain a reasonable standard of living.

18. Gorringe, *Capital and the Kingdom*, 167.
19. Gorringe, "Can Bankers Be Saved?" 29.

At the same time, it is possible to hold that this unhappiness with interest was not only related to interest owed by poor people but to all interest on loans. Here a major concern was obviously with the effects of interest on poor people, but it could go much further to the effects of interest on society as a whole. From our perspective, it is unfortunate that these concerns are not spelled out for us either in the Scriptures or in the Fathers. Perhaps it was all too obvious—how money and other resources became concentrated in the hands of a few, how there was a temptation for those with money to seek even more, rather than use it for productive activity. Perhaps also there were echoes of the suspicions felt outside the Jewish and Christian faiths—illustrated by the restriction of interest in some ancient law codes, by the brief prohibition of interest in the Roman Empire in 342 BC, and by the writings of Aristotle. Perhaps there was even suspicion of how interest can result in rising prices, or of the particular dangers of compound interest—how the amount of debt to be repaid can grow and grow while the resources to repay it stand still or go backwards.

It can be argued (as I shall do shortly) that an interest-free economy would be a much more equitable economy than the capitalist economy of today. It would also bring the money economy much closer to the real economy of production and selling. On the other hand, based on the fact that Israelites *were* allowed to lend and borrow at interest in dealings with non-Israelites (at least, those based outside Israel), it could be argued that a small amount of interest could be legitimate on commercial transactions in order to make such transactions worthwhile. What would be required in our day would be some worldwide regulation on the matter. In this case, one would be treating the Old Testament usury prohibition, as suggested by Richard Higginson, as a "paradigm" rather than a "model." A paradigm, he suggests, is an *example* of a principle in action: "We must take the principle to heart and seek to apply it, but the form in which we do that in our modern society will probably differ from the way in which it is articulated in the Bible."[20] The same kind of argument could be made in regard to the debt-cancellation provision in the Torah—that this enshrines a fundamental principle about the dangers involved in long-term debt, which we need to take seriously, even if the way we apply it today might differ from that enshrined in the Torah.

20. Higginson, *Called to Account*, 113.

The important thing from our point of view is that these dangers in the use of money can, in fact, be seen in the current world economy.

Generally speaking, writers on economics have been singularly unwilling to grapple with the detrimental consequences of interest. Paul Mills, however, in his paper, *The Ban on Interest: Dead Letter or Radical Solution?* has succinctly listed the following negative effects of interest:

1. The unjust and destabilizing allocation of returns between the users and suppliers of finance

2. The misallocation of finance to the safest borrowers rather than to the most productive

3. A propensity to finance speculation in assets and property

4. An inherently unstable banking system

5. A short-termist investment strategy

6. A concentration of wealth into fewer and fewer hands

7. A rapid flow of financial capital across regions and countries[21]

Some would add an eighth consequence—that interest (especially compound interest) is a major cause of inflation, because interest repayments enable banks to make more loans, putting more money into the economy, and this leads to rising prices.[22] James Robertson points out that the cost of interest repayments forms a substantial part of the cost of all goods and services—which, unless counteracted by reductions in other costs, will inevitably produce higher prices.[23] Mills points to the extra effects of the fact that most interest payments are at compound interest.

I have already drawn attention to the fact that, unless there is increasing productivity (perhaps through the introduction of improved technology or reductions in the labor force) or an expanding market, an economy built on debt necessarily has to keep on growing in order to produce profits—and this applies even more with interest. The danger is the development of a spiral of debt that can get out of hand. From the same point of view, if growth starts to fall, it can lead to a downward spiral. As there is usually a time lag between production and sale, firms have to take on further loans to cover the income shortfall and the interest payments

21. Mills, *The Ban on Interest*, 4–7.
22. Kennedy, *Interest and Inflation-Free Money*.
23. Robertson, *Future Wealth*, 124.

on previous loans. To keep the economy growing (unless there are productivity increases) producers have to produce more and more items for sale, which are often of poor quality with built-in obsolescence, needing to be sold with heavy advertising, or are luxury items for which there is no urgent need. The ultimate end of such activity is the using up of the earth's resources to little useful effect.

Mills goes further in *Interest in Interest*, where he suggests positive effects of an interest-free system. He suggests, first of all, that in the medieval period the ban on lending at interest encouraged the spirit of enterprise and risk-taking investment, moving capital out of speculation into commerce. Since banks would not be allowed to lend at interest, they would have, instead, to invest and set up partnership arrangements with companies, one result of which would be to avoid the risky lending arrangements that have been so common recently. The profits of such arrangements would be shared between the banks and their partners—as also the losses—which would have the effect of reducing bankruptcies and encouraging enterprise. As much as anything, however, the chief benefit would be much greater stability in the whole system, banks would be safer because of their avoidance of speculative risk, and business cycles would be less dramatic. In the political realm, it could have the effect of reducing the dominance of the financial sector and increasing public control.[24]

That this is not the pious thinking of a Christian academic may be illustrated perhaps with a reference to John Maynard Keynes, who wrote in his *General Theory of Employment, Interest and Money*:

> Provisions against usury are amongst the most ancient economic practices of which we have record. The destruction of the inducement to invest by an excessive liquidity-preference was the outstanding evil, the prime impediment to the growth of wealth, in the ancient and medieval worlds. And naturally so, since certain of the risks and hazards of economic life diminish the marginal efficiency of capital whilst others serve to increase the preference for liquidity. In a world, therefore, which no one reckoned to be safe, it was almost inevitable that the rate of interest, unless it was curbed by every instrument at the disposal of society, would rise too high to permit of an adequate inducement to invest. I was brought up to believe that the attitude of the Medieval Church to

24. Mills, *Interest in Interest*, 36–37.

the rate of interest was inherently absurd, and that the subtle discussions aimed at distinguishing the return on money-loans from the return to active investment were merely jesuistical attempts to find a practical escape from a foolish theory. But I now read these discussions as an honest intellectual effort to keep separate what the classical theory has inextricably confused together, namely, the rate of interest and the marginal efficiency of capital. For it now seems clear that the disquisitions of the schoolmen were directed towards the elucidation of a formula which should allow the schedule of the marginal efficiency of capital to be high, whilst using rule and custom to keep down the rate of interest.[25]

Elsewhere Keynes speculated that an economy run at full employment could reduce the rate of return on capital to zero within a generation.[26] This would mean "the euthanasia of the rentier, and, consequently, the euthanasia of the cumulative oppressive power of the capitalist to exploit the scarcity-value of capital"[27]—which he regarded as a welcome prospect. He certainly saw no absolute necessity for the payment of interest on money loans. Mills suggests that "the funeral has been postponed by the internationalization and deregulation of world financial markets, rapid technological innovation and persistent debt-financing by governments,"[28] but believes (as we have already seen) that there are, nevertheless, many undesirable features of market economies that can be attributed to the existence of interest.[29]

Over the years there have been various proposals about the way in which interest could be eliminated. These usually center on preventing commercial banks from creating money and requiring that central banks issue money free of interest. Margrit Kennedy develops the ideas of Silvio Gessell, who proposed that governments issue money free of interest and that users of money pay a "use fee" to the government if they don't use it.[30] The area in which the prohibition of interest on money loans has actually been tried, of course, is in Islamic finance. Even here there can be differences between banks (and the scholars on whose opinions they

25. Keynes, *General Theory of Employment, Interest and Money*, 351–52.

26. Ibid., 220 and 275.

27. Ibid., 276.

28. Mills, "Should Interest Exist?" 66.

29. Ibid., 182.

30. Kennedy, *Interest and Inflation-Free Money*, 21–24

depend), rather as the scholastics disagreed in their pronouncements on various financial instruments. Generally speaking, however, there is a strong rejection of the creation of money as debt, and a strong emphasis on commercial partnerships rather than loans.[31] As a result of the financial crisis that began in 2007, there is renewed interest in the subject. In a supplement to *The Times* devoted to Islamic Finance on November 27, 2008, it was reported that global Islamic banking had been relatively unscathed by the crisis, and that the Financial Services Agency believed that Islamic finance would play an important role in the future of UK financial services.

To reduce or remove the influence of interest would fly in the face of all secular thinking about money since the Middle Ages—and a great majority of Christian thinking. No doubt, it could be very difficult to turn such thinking into legislation. On the other hand, the financial crisis that began in 2007 has been so severe (there was one weekend in September 2008 when the whole financial system seemed on the verge of collapse) that there may emerge a new willingness to consider such radical ideas. It is still possible, in fact, that, even if the measures that have been taken (relying so much on an enormous increase in interest-bearing debt) have removed the immediate danger to the system, these very measures may produce an economy fraught with just as much danger as the pre-2007 situation, and a similar or even worse crisis could arise. It could be said that now is the time for Christian writers to speak out forcefully from the heart of their tradition a word that will challenge the basic orthodoxies on which the present system is founded—not just the greed that bankers and others have demonstrated, but those features of the system that allow money to exercise an unfettered role and, in so doing, to cause as much harm as the good it also produces. And a major feature of this system is lending at interest.

31. Mills himself has written on Islamic finance, in Mills and Presley: *Islamic Finance: Theory and Practice.* This is a sympathetic treatment of Islamic practice, giving an assessment of its advantages as a non-interest financial system, while recognizing the difficulties there would be in extending it worldwide. A more recent treatment is that of Tarek El Diwany, *The Problem with Interest*, which covers the whole ground, while dealing more extensively with the general problems produced by interest.

SECTION THREE

Evaluating Money

CHAPTER FOUR

Money and Justice

HAVING CONSIDERED SOME BASIC uses of money, in lending and borrowing, and discovered the serious problems that an unregulated use of money produces, I turn in the next four chapters to an evaluation of money from four points of view that are generally ignored by those who have a positive or neutral view of it—not least, those who have embraced a neoliberal philosophy. In each case, I will be demonstrating how money in its very nature creates enormous problems—problems that are highlighted in the tradition of Christian theology.

I turn first to demonstrate how the use of money almost inevitably produces injustice. As before, the claim is not that love of money produces injustice (though it does), so much as money in itself. A situation of injustice I understand to be one of inequality, one in which a person's experience bears no relation to either one's needs, deserts, or rights.

From a historical point of view, this problem was already evident in antiquity. In his study of the introduction of the first coined money, Richard Seaforth interprets it as a critical element in the sidelining of the Greek gods and the development of the Greek city-state. Having pointed out how exchange for money produced an equality between the parties involved (which had not normally been present in the era of gift-exchange), he goes on to say:

> However, money and the growth of trade introduce a new form of instability. Equality between the parties in respect of the exchange does nothing to prevent the *unlimited* impoverishment or enrichment that had been precluded by the old assymetrical relations of positive reciprocity and redistribution. It was precisely this new form of instability, in which eventually the rich enslave the poor, that Solon [in Athens] was appointed to resolve.[1]

1. Seaford, *Money and the Early Greek Mind*, 197.

Seaforth then points out how the introduction of money "tends to marginalise reciprocity, and permits an unprecedented appearance of individual autonomy," and how "the power of money can increase human independence even from deity."[2]

In general terms, this points to the conclusion that money *in its very nature* (unless it is controlled by state regulation) leads irresistibly to inequality and injustice. Essentially, money, after it has been created, is held by individuals (or by corporate bodies) rather than by the community as a whole. If all property were shared, there would be no need for it. But as soon as money is created, it tends to be used for the benefit of the individual, rather than for the community as a whole. This is not to say that money should not be used, but to indicate a serious danger in its use. Over history this is one reason that states have imposed taxes—not just to boost their treasuries, but to redistribute what seems, inevitably, to fall into fewer and fewer hands and endanger the livelihood of the remainder.

The social problems produced by poverty are well documented. In a celebrated recent book, Richard Wilkinson and Kate Pickett go one step further to show that these problems can actually be produced in societies (even rich societies) where there is a marked degree of inequality between those at the top of the ladder and those at the bottom. They go even further to suggest that a more equal society is better for everyone in it.[3] This chapter intends to demonstrate how the connection between money and inequality has been appreciated in the tradition of Christian theology.

Justice in the Jewish Law

When we look at early Jewish life, we see that it was characterized by a strong sense of community, and that the Law of Moses, which came to govern that life, was aimed at the sustenance of all members of the community, and especially of the poor. If anyone became poor for any reason (i.e., they were not able to maintain themselves with the necessities of life), others were required to help them in any way possible (Leviticus 25:35–43; Deuteronomy 15:7–11)—and there was a whole string of ordinances to make life easier for the poor (for instance in Leviticus 19 and Deuteronomy 24). It is boldly stated in Deuteronomy 15:4–6 that, if the

2. Ibid.

3. Wilkinson and Pickett, *The Spirit Level: Why Equality Is Better for Everyone.*

people fully obey the ordinances of the law, "there should be no poor among you." Recognizing, however, that "there will always be poor people in the land," verses 7–11 encourage Israelites to lend generously to one another without expecting anything in return. Then after seven years, of course, there was the general cancellation of debts.

Despite all this emphasis on helping the poor, it is important to state that the Jewish law does not imply a negative attitude toward riches in themselves. In fact, throughout the Torah, God repeatedly promised his people that obedience would bring abundant prosperity in a land flowing with milk and honey (e.g., Deuteronomy 6:1–3). Deuteronomy 28:1–14 lists a whole series of blessings that will follow obedience. "You will lend to many nations, but will borrow from none" (v. 12). Wealth and riches were not to be despised. What was required was that they be enjoyed with *righteousness* (or justice; Hebrew *tsedekah*).

Tsedekah was regarded as one of the great characteristics of Yahweh (Isaiah 5:16). Sometimes this has been interpreted in overly legalistic terms. Since the time of von Rad, however, it has been recognized that righteousness needs to be understood primarily in terms of relationship: "Every relationship brings with it certain claims upon conduct, and the satisfaction of these claims, which issue from the relationship and in which alone the relationship can persist, is described by our term *tsedekah*."[4] God's righteousness, therefore, was demonstrated in his actions to establish and preserve the relationship of covenant between himself and his people.

Likewise, his people were to show the same righteousness among themselves.[5] This was not so much a question of fulfilling legal requirements as of living out the relationship that was inherent in being God's people. In the words of Walter Brueggemann, "Israel regards itself as a community of persons bound in membership to each other, so that each person-as-member is to be treated well enough to be sustained as a full member of the community."[6] Altogether, the program of the Torah was aimed at producing a society in which everybody was able to enjoy the necessities of life (and very much more). The ideal picture was of "each man [sitting] under his own vine and fig tree" (1 Kings 4:25; Micah 4:4;

---

4. von Rad, *Old Testament Theology*, 1:371.
5. Birch, *Let Justice Roll Down*, 259–60.
6. Brueggemann, *Theology of the Old Testament*, 421.

Zechariah 3:10). The picture was certainly not of some individuals possessing large sums of money while others suffered in poverty. Even if there is only sketchy evidence of some of the laws actually being implemented, what we have in the Torah is a remarkable picture of the ideal that Jewish teachers held before their people, and to which they held over a very long period.

In contrast with the present capitalist system, therefore, though there was a general presumption that contracts must be honored and that debts must be paid, these presuppositions were not absolute, so that, where it was felt that the welfare of the community required that exceptions be made, then the Law made appropriate provisions. Similarly, although there was a general presumption of the sanctity of private property (illustrated by the seventh commandment, "Thou shalt not steal"), it was still appreciated that everything belonged to God (as in 1 Chronicles 29:10–13) and that possessions were not for selfish use, but rather for the benefit of all.

Justice in the Prophets

The evidence of the book of Judges suggests that this period was by no means a golden era when the Law (as they knew it) was fully observed. What is certain, however, is that the establishment of the monarchy changed everything—as Samuel had predicted (1 Samuel 8:10–18). Much of the land came into the ownership of the king, and, following the practice of surrounding peoples, was allocated by him to his officials, soldiers, and other favorites. One may assume also that this was a period of rapid growth in the money economy. Israel became heavily involved in international trade, with King Solomon owning a large fleet of ships, with which he traded with countries far away to the east (1 Kings 9:26–28; 10:22). For the ordinary people, however, life became very difficult. Despite any laws that there may have been against giving loans at interest, or of taking fellow Jews into slavery, many found themselves at the mercy of the king and other large landowners. (In the kingdom idealized in Ezekiel 40–48, the king is only allocated a limited portion of the land; 45:7–9.)

A good example of this injustice is the case of Naboth's vineyard in 1 Kings 21, where King Ahab set his heart on the vineyard of a poor subject; his wife persuaded him to make false accusations against Naboth; Ahab had him condemned to death, and then took his land for himself. This was the portion of land allocated to Naboth's family for generations, but the king, on a whim, felt able to take it from him. No wonder the prophet Elijah rebuked the king so strongly. In the case of both Elijah and Elisha (the major prophets of the early part of the monarchy), while their protests were primarily against the worship of foreign gods, there was also a definite concern about the plight of the poor (as seen especially in 2 Kings 4) and the injustice involved.

John Bright says, "Israel's distinctive social structure had completely lost its character. . . . The rise of the monarchy, with the attendant organization of life under the crown, had transferred the effective basis of social organization to the state and, together with the burgeoning of commercial activity, had created a privileged class, weakened tribal ties, and destroyed the solidarity characteristic of tribal society."[7] And in the words of Walter Brueggemann, "Covenanting that takes brothers and sisters seriously had been replaced by consuming."[8]

As an example of the prophets whose words have come down to us in writing, we may take the prophet Amos, preaching in the eighth century in the northern kingdom of Israel. The reign of Jeroboam (like that of Solomon) was a time of great prosperity, but Amos saw it as riddled with apostasy and injustice. In some of the strongest language used by a prophet, he was particularly angry at the oppression of the poor by the rich:

> Hear this, you who trample the needy
>   and do away with the poor of the land,
>   saying
> "When will the New Moon be over
>   that we may sell grain,
>   and the Sabbath be ended
>   that we may market wheat?"—
> skimping the measure,
>   boosting the price,
>   and cheating with dishonest scales,
> buying the poor with silver
>   and the needy for a pair of sandals,
>   selling even the sweepings with the wheat. (Amos 8:4–6)

7. Bright, *A History of Israel*, 241–42.
8. Brueggemann, *The Prophetic Imagination*, 27.

Here are some of the specific requirements of the law being clearly repudiated: insisting on the repayment of a debt, rather than showing generosity (Deuteronomy 15:7–11), judging unfairly (Leviticus 19:15);,taking bribes (Exodus 23:8), taking fellow Israelites into slavery (Leviticus 25:39), and using unfair measures in trading (Deuteronomy 25:13–16). God's response is clear and to the point: "I will not listen to the music of your harps, *but let justice roll on like a river, and righteousness like a never-failing stream!*" (Amos 5:23–24, my italics).

The period of the exile was marked by a serious study of the Law and the rise of a group of "scribes" dedicated to passing it on, and these exercised great influence among the people. The renewing of the covenant under Ezra in the fifth century is often regarded as a turning point in the history of the people. In the words of John Bright, "Ezra was, in any event, a figure of towering importance. . . . If Moses was Israel's founder, it was Ezra who reconstituted Israel and gave her faith a form in which it could survive through the centuries."[9] It is clear, however, that carrying out the Law still remained a problem. In the book of Nehemiah (around the time of Ezra's ministry) we can still read the complaints of ordinary people that they are caught between paying tribute to the Persian government and the exactions of their Jewish brothers:

> We are mortgaging our fields, our vineyards and our homes to get grain during the famine. . . . Although we are the same flesh and blood as our countrymen and though our sons are as good as theirs, yet we have to subject our sons and daughters to slavery. Some of our daughters have already been enslaved, but we are powerless, because our fields and our vineyards belong to others. (Nehemiah 5:3–5)

Nehemiah replies, "Give back to them immediately their fields, vineyards, olive groves and houses, and also the usury you are charging them—the hundredth part of the money, grain, new wine and oil" (5:11)—giving us the one example we have of the sort of general debt relief envisaged in the Law for the sabbatical year. It is likely, however, that this provided only temporary relief. "Realistically," says Gottwald, "since the wealth of the abusive upper class was not confiscated, the combination of landed and commercial wealth probably worked toward the eventual undermining of the reforms in Judah, as proved to be the case in Athens after Solon's reforms."[10]

9. Bright, *A History of Israel*, 374.

10. Gottwald, *The Tribes of Judah*, 433.

What the prophets did hold on to, however, was that one day God would send a king who would rule in righteousness and justice. This would be a decisive intervention by God in the affairs of the world. As time went by, and oppressive rule by foreigners became the norm, this hope became widespread in Israel. It was centered in the minds of the people on the coming of a Davidic king (or Messiah) who would rule in righteousness.[11]

Justice in the New Testament

By the time of Jesus, Jewish society was dominated by a number of large families who owned much of the land and controlled most of the levers of power. They might have represented only 2 percent of the population, but by judicious use of patronage and the cultivation of clients and control of the judicial system, the temple, and the military, they were able to exercise an almost absolute control over the majority peasant people.[12] Except insofar as they were drawn into the cities (like Sepphoris, Tiberias, or Jerusalem) to serve the interests of the aristocratic families, the ordinary people lived mainly in small villages (like Nazareth or Bethlehem) and worked in the fields, many on the aristocratic estates. Agriculture was flourishing at this time, but distribution of the produce was almost entirely in the hands of the aristocrats, so that their workers often lived in considerable poverty. As things were, however, it was generally fruitless to revolt or try to change the system. The best they could do was to work the system, as much as possible, to their own advantage, or engage in armed banditry. The one group that did attempt revolution were the Zealots. Founded by Judas the Galilean, who led a revolt against Rome in AD 6, they continued to be a thorn in the side of the Romans until Masada, their last stronghold, fell in AD 74.[13]

After many centuries during which the subject of the kingdom of God was virtually ignored by scholars, at the end of the nineteenth century it became a matter of central theological interest, largely through

11. Russell, *Between the Testaments*, 119–41. Note also the characters of Simeon and Anna in Luke 2, who were looking eagerly for "the consolation of Israel" (2:25) and "the redemption of Jerusalem" (2:38).

12. Hanson and Oakman, *Palestine in the Time of Jesus*, 70–82.

13. Ferguson, *Backgrounds of Early Christianity*, 421–22; Josephus, *Jewish Wars* 7.8–9.

the work of Albrecht Ritschl, and it came to be appreciated that, when Jesus came, this was the central focus of his preaching. Initially, the emphasis of scholars was on the eschatological aspect of the kingdom—that it was not a matter of this-worldly moral improvement, but the miracle of God's intervention in human history for salvation and for judgment. As time passed, however, greater emphasis was placed on the present experience of the kingdom.[14] Gradually, a basic consensus has developed, which (in the words of Bruce Chilton) could be described as follows: "Jesus' message of the kingdom referred fundamentally and distinctively to a transcendent reality, not to any human organisation. The kingdom is not a movement or a regime, but the sovereign activity of God. More particularly, the kingdom is to be understood within an appreciation of eschatology: what Jesus announced was nothing less than the ultimate intervention of God in human affairs, the tangible end of the world."[15] Included in this consensus is the idea of "realised eschatology," a term coined by C. H. Dodd—that the ultimate fulfillment of the kingdom is yet to come, but that it is made visible in the ministry of Jesus.

The ministry of Jesus reveals a clear understanding by him of the plight of the poor (all those deprived in any way of the world's resources) and of God's desire that, in his kingdom, measures should be taken to deal with it. This was not a new revelation of God's desire, but (in sending his Son) God was taking drastic action (as implied in Mark 12:6), and Jesus demonstrated in both his life and teaching that success would not be achieved by a mere tinkering with the status quo. What was required was a radical reorientation of society in which people no longer sought their own prosperity but the prosperity of all.

It has been claimed by several writers that Jesus was a political messiah, seeking (even if by nonviolent means), to replace the rule of Rome with the kingdom of God.[16] If this is meant to mean that Jesus was the kind of political messiah that many of the Jews were expecting, then it has to be said that Jesus refused on many occasions to accept this expectation—e.g., in the temptations in the wilderness (Matthew 4:4; Luke 4:4), in his refusal to be made king following the Feeding of the Five Thousand (John 6:15), and in his reply to Pilate: "My kingdom is not of this world.

---

14. Chilton, *Kingdom of God*, 1–26.

15. Ibid., 25–26.

16. Myers, *Binding the Strong Man*; Herzog, *Parables as Subversive Speech*.

If it were, my servants would fight to prevent my arrest by the Jews. But now my kingdom is from another place" (John 18:36). From the records we have, Jesus was not encouraging revolt against the occupying power. Even Myers makes clear that Jesus advocated nonviolence. (He shows how Mark 13:14–16 was taken by the early Christians to mean that they were not to join in the Jewish revolt that began in AD 66.)[17]

On the other hand, Jesus's teaching did have very radical implications, which could have been interpreted as subversive.[18] What is certain is that Jesus's advocacy of the kingdom of God was understood as subversive by those who controlled the levers of power in Jerusalem, and that they accused him of being a rival to the Roman power (Luke 23:2). The ethic preached by him was very different from that practiced by the elites of his day. Hanson and Oakman are correct to say that "Jesus' alternative is first and foremost an expression of non-elite interests and aspirations."[19] Above all, however, we see in the teaching of Jesus an ethical program very similar to that of the Torah and a desire for its implementation. Just as the Torah gives a program for an ideal Jewish society, in which the needs of all are met, so the ethics of the kingdom of God in the teaching of Jesus are a radical program for an egalitarian society based on his interpretation of the Torah.[20]

As soon as Jesus returned to heaven (Acts 1:9), and the Holy Spirit had fallen on his disciples (2:1–4), the picture we are given of the first Christians in Jerusalem includes a sharing of goods that clearly reflects the ideal of Deuteronomy 15:4: "There should be no poor among you." Despite the widespread opinion that this represented a full-blooded "Christian communism," this was probably not a total sharing of goods. What is recorded is that those with land and houses sold them and placed the money at the apostles' feet, and it was distributed to anyone as they had need (4:34–35). Such measures to help the weaker members of the Christian community continued throughout the New Testament period. In Acts 11:27–30, the church in Antioch, on learning about a severe

17. Myers, *Binding the Strong Man*, 335–36.

18. In Jesus' "tribute to Caesar" reply, Myers suggests that he was definitely encouraging refusal to pay the hated poll tax (310–12).

19. Hanson and Oakman, *Palestine in the Time of Jesus*, 125.

20. I am taking the biblical texts as they stand, accepting that, in this way, we are discovering what was accepted as the teaching of Jesus by those who settled the New Testament canon.

famine that would spread over the whole Roman world, sent help to the poor Christians living in Judea.

Towards the end of his ministry, St. Paul gave a great deal of time and energy to taking a collection among other churches on behalf of the church in Jerusalem. In this project he was particularly concerned to cement the unity of Jewish and Gentile Christians in one worldwide church, but there was clearly an ongoing need in Jerusalem. Paul urged his readers to be generous in their response. At the same time, he felt it went further than this, arguing that to act in this way would produce an *equality*: "At the present time your plenty will provide what they need, so that in turn their plenty will supply what you need. Then there will be an equality" (2 Corinthians 8:14). And he went on to quote what happened when the people were given the manna in the wilderness: "He who gathered much did not have too much, and he who gathered little did not have too little" (2 Corinthians 8:15).

Justice in the Church Fathers

While my concern in this book is with the question of money, it must be recognized that the money people possess is but one aspect of their possessions, so that "mammon," as I have suggested, may refer not only to money, but to the whole of a person's property, whatever that may be. For many people over much of history money has not been the most important aspect of their possessions. More significant has been the land they farmed and the house in which they lived. Of great significance, therefore, in the five hundred years' dominance of the Roman Empire is the concept of property rights that they set in stone, which has since been extended throughout the world, and forms the basis of the modern capitalist economy. The roots were there in the city-states of ancient Greece,[21] and were spreading under Alexander the Great and his successors.[22] However, it was in the formidable strength of Roman law that it became so institutionalized that most of the empire's citizens came to take it for granted.

In communities throughout the world, land was originally held in common, even where (as in Israel) it was allocated for use to different clans and families. In the case of Israel, we have already seen how more

21. Duchrow and Hinkelammert, *Property for People, Not for Profit*, 7–10.
22. Ibid., 10–11.

and more of the land was taken over by the state and by large aristo-cratic families. All of this was formalized under Roman Law, in what is commonly called the absolute conception of ownership—which was "the unrestricted right of control over a physical thing, and whosoever has this right can claim the thing he owns, wherever it is, and no matter who pos-sesses it."[23] Such ownership was sacrosanct, even if the original obtaining of the ownership was by violence, war, or theft. More often, as we have seen, it could be acquired in payment of a debt. Of course, it could also be bought and sold in a legally acceptable way.[24]

As time went by, this system came to be taken for granted. Even the plebeians seem to have accepted it, because it gave them secure ownership of the small pieces of land they farmed. There were occasional peasant revolts, put down brutally by the Roman armies. More often, disgruntled peasants would just leave the countryside and flee to the towns—where, of course, they would be beggars or, if possible, paid laborers. Possessing no land, they would have no political power, and many would become slaves. For these people money (as a commodity) became more impor-tant. However, the importance of money would not increase dramatically until urbanization really took off.[25] This being so, it may not surprise us that there is little discussion about money (in itself) in the first part of this period, but much more about property and possessions.

As the church grew, it felt the need for an orderly presentation of the faith, both for members and nonmembers. There grew up, therefore, a number of catechetical schools, of which the most famous was at Alex-andria, whose most illustrious teacher was Clement (ca. AD 150–215). Clement developed several ideas that were significant in this period. *Autarkeia* (or self-sufficiency) was a popular idea in Greek philosophy, producing, it was said, freedom from anxiety. For Clement, however, self-sufficiency should not be seen as a license for amassing riches for one's own benefit. For him, if one possessed property, this was not an end in itself; all one needed was what was sufficient to meet the necessities of

23. Jolovicz and Nichols, *Historical Introduction to the Study of Roman Law*, 140.

24. Avila, *Ownership*, 20.

25. Ironically, the insistence of the upper classes on maintaining their large estates and refusing to break them up, even when large tracts were no longer farmed, has been seen by some as a strong contribution to the eventual collapse of the empire. "The Ro-man Law theory and practice of absolute and exclusive ownership of land had been tried now—and for more than a millennium—and been found altogether wanting" (Ibid., 32).

life; after that, it was an opportunity for sharing with others who were less fortunate (*koinonia*). In this, he was clearly opposing the Roman idea that ownership of property was absolute. Instead of doing what you liked with your possessions, you should be seeking to do what God wills.

Most significant from our point of view is Clement's homily on Mark 10:17–31 (the Rich Young Ruler)—entitled *Quis ho sosomenos plousios?* ("Who is the Rich Man that is Saved?"). Clement interprets Jesus's words in this passage, not as a condemnation of all rich people who retain their riches, but rather as a condemnation of those who are so attached to their riches that they are unwilling to let them go. In fact, he interprets "unrighteous mammon" (in Luke 16:9) as meaning that all possessions are by nature unrighteous "when a man possesses them for personal advantage as being entirely his own, and does not bring them into the common stock for those in need"; but then claims that "from this unrighteousness it is possible to perform a deed that is righteous and saving, namely, to give relief to one of those who have an eternal habitation with the Father."[26] In this way, Clement avoids the two extremes of complete renunciation of riches and the Roman concept of absolute ownership. For him, it is obvious that people need material goods; otherwise they would be tempted to steal and to other improper means of acquiring them. In fact material goods are the generous gift of God to meet our needs. They are not given, however, for selfish indulgence; rather, to minister to the needs of all.

The fortunes of the church took a decisive turn with the conversion of Constantine, his accession as head of the western half of the empire in 312, and the eventual recognition of Christianity as the religion of the empire. In this new situation Christians and the church began to acquire extensive property, and there was a real temptation to use this for selfish purposes. Despite this (or because of it) we see a continuance of the same attitude to possessions in the leading Fathers. Among the writers of this new period, we can turn to Basil the Great (330–379) who became bishop of Caesarea in Cappadocia in 370. Cappadocia at this time was a land of peasants, who farmed the great estates of (often absent) landowners. Although himself the owner of much property, Basil distributed all his possessions to the poor and became a monk. As bishop he was greatly concerned about the riches of the few amidst the poverty of the many,

26. Migne, *Patrologia Graeca* 9:637, translation by Butterworth of Clement of Alexandria, *The Exhortation to the Greeks, The Rich Man's Salvation, To the Newly Baptized*, 337.

and, of all the early Fathers, he came closest to denying the right to private property:

> Whom do I injure [the rich man says] when I retain and conserve my own? Which things, tell me, are yours? Whence have you brought them into being? You are like one occupying a place in the theatre, who should prohibit others from entering, requiring as one's own which was designed for the common use of all. Such are the rich. Because they were the first to occupy common goods, they take these goods as their own. If each one would take what is sufficient for one's needs, leaving what is in excess to those in distress, no-one would be rich, and no-one poor. . . . Are you not avaricious? Are you not a robber? You who make your own the things which you have received to distribute. Will not one be called a thief who steals the garment of one already clothed, and is one deserving of any other title who will not clothe the naked if he is able to do so?[27]

I conclude with Augustine of Hippo (354–430), probably the most significant doctor of the church in the first four centuries. He was baptized in 387, having been much influenced by Ambrose. He then returned from Milan to Africa, where he sold his goods and gave the proceeds to the poor, moving onto one of his former estates to found a small monastic community. On becoming a bishop, he turned his bishop's residence into a similar community. His ethical teaching begins with his famous maxim, *solo Deo fruendum*, "only God is to be enjoyed." Material things are rather to be "used," as God wills, and not "abused." Possession of material goods can only be justified if they are used rightly. "The one who uses his wealth badly possesses it wrongfully, and wrongful possession means that it is another's property."[28] "The superfluous things of the wealthy are the necessities of the poor. When superfluous things are possessed [selfishly], others' property is possessed."[29]

In saying this, Augustine seems to accept the legal right of private property, while claiming that (ethically) it is only rightly owned if it is shared. He regards private property, in fact, as the chief enemy of peace,

---

27. Basil the Great, *Homily on "I will pull down my barns"* (Migne, *Patrologia Graeca* 31:276–77); in Avila, *Ownership*, 49–50.

28. Augustine, *Letters* 153.26 (Migne, *Patrologia Latina* 33:665); in Avila, *Ownership*, 110.

29. Augustine, *Homily on Psalm 147* (Migne, *Patrologia Latina* 37:1922); in Avila, *Ownership*, 113.

leading to selfishness and concentration on material things, and as being destructive of community. "Let us, therefore, abstain from the possession of private property—or from the love of it, if we cannot abstain from possession—and let us make room for God. . . . In property which each possesses privately, each necessarily becomes proud."[30]

Justice in the Scholastics

Understanding the scholastics' view of money has to begin with a realization that they were definitely motivated by a *moral* concern—to decide what exchanges were right and what were wrong. Aquinas's most extended treatment of money is found, for instance, in the section of the *Summa Theologica* devoted to "vices opposed to justice."[31] More precisely, it is to be found in the section on vices opposed to *commutative* justice—which was concerned with the question of *equality* in exchange—which required perfect equality between whatever items were exchanged.[32] To act in accordance with commutative justice was a virtue; to act contrary to it was a vice. Where money was involved, the aim should be to discover "the just price" for each transaction.

The question of the just price is treated by Aquinas in the *Summa Theologica*, part II, 2nd part, question 77 ("Whether it is lawful to sell a thing for more than it's worth"). This very question suggests that Aquinas felt there was a figure (even if a rough one) that would indicate the just price for any particular transaction. He wrote, "the just price of things is not fixed with mathematical precision, but depends on a kind of estimate, so that a slight addition or subtraction would not seem to destroy the equality of justice."[33] At the same time, he didn't seem to know exactly how this price was made up. He certainly accepted that the seller's labor and risk have something to do with it. He said, "A tradesman . . . may lawfully (sell at an increased price) either because he has bettered the thing or because the value of the thing has changed with the change of place or time, or on account of the danger he incurs in transferring the thing

30. Augustine, *Homilies on Luke* 7.124 (Migne, *Patrologia Latina* 15:1731); in Avila, *Ownership*, 120.

31. English translation of the title.

32. Aquinas, *Summa Theologica*, part II, 2nd part, q. 77, art. 1, pp. 318–19.

33. Ibid., q. 77, art. 1, p. 320.

from one place to another."[34] He also recognized that supply could make a difference (in his story of a wheat-seller approaching a city just before others who would drive the price down).[35]

Similarly with the question of usury (which I have already discussed)—this was reckoned as a matter of justice. It was reckoned that, since a fungible was consumed in use, it was not possible (in a fungible) to separate ownership from use. But, in the case of a loan at interest, it could be argued that such a separation was taking place. So Aquinas himself wrote, in his classic definition of usury:

> In suchlike things the use of the thing must not be reckoned apart from the thing itself, and whoever is granted the use of the thing, is granted the thing itself; and for this reason, to lend things of this kind is to transfer the ownership. Accordingly, if a man wanted to sell wine separately from the use of wine, he would be selling the same thing twice, or he would be selling what does not exist, wherefore he would evidently commit a sin of injustice. In like manner, he commits an injustice who lends wine or wheat, and asks for double payment—viz. (1) the return of the thing in equal measure (2) the price of the use, which is called usury.[36]

Aquinas's great point here is that to sell the same thing twice (in its substance and its use) is against natural justice. In relation to usury, he does quote biblical passages like Exodus 22:25 and accepts the later warnings of the prophets that the Jews should abstain from *all* lending at interest.[37] It is, however, from the condemnation of natural justice that most of his conclusions are drawn. Some of these arguments from natural justice may seem far-fetched and abstruse to us today. They even lend weight to the way in which the scholastics have been pilloried as those who argue about how many angels can dance on the end of a pin. It is important for us to realize, however, that their discussions about money did have very practical outcomes, and the discussions emerged from trying to deal with very practical problems. The problem of usury, for instance, was not just an issue of concern to bankers and merchants. It affected anyone who needed to borrow or lend, and, to the scholastics, was a profoundly ethical issue.

34. Ibid., art. 4, p. 328.
35. Ibid., art. 3, p. 326.
36. Ibid., q. 78, art. 1, pp. 330–31.
37. Aquinas, *De Malo*, answer to question 13; in Davies, *A History of Money*, 739.

Lester Little points out the irony that these scholastics, who were taken mainly from the Franciscan and Dominican orders, founded on the absolute poverty of their members, should be those to formulate an ethic that often justified the activities of those groups immersed in the making of money.[38] Odd Langholm is more generous. He describes the efforts of the scholastics as an attempt "to face up to the dilemmas and contradictions involved in the concept of a Christian economy."[39] The result, he admits, is a compromise: "It grants the social benefits of man's avarice to a certain extent, while appealing, insistently and consistently, to his benevolence."[40] R. H. Tawney gives his own summary:

> The significance of [the movement's] contribution . . . is to be found in the insistence of medieval thinkers that society is a spiritual organism, not an economic machine, and that economic activity . . . requires to be controlled and repressed by reference to the moral ends for which it supplies the material means. . . . The experiment may have been impracticable, and almost from the first it was discredited by the notorious corruption of ecclesiastical authorities, who preached renunciation and gave a lesson in greed. But it had in it something of the heroic, and to ignore the nobility of the conception is not less absurd than to idealize its practical results.[41]

In the end, perhaps, the failure of scholasticism to settle issues in the economic sphere is simply a reflection of the inability of the church to maintain control over all aspects of life. The attempt to establish Christendom was, from this point of view, a unique phenomenon in social history, which it is difficult to imagine ever being seen again.

Justice in the Early Modern Period

Diana Wood describes the twelfth century as the century of the "discovery of the individual," particularly perhaps as there was pressure on rural land, and individuals began to acquire property in towns.[42] Augustine had allowed private property as long as it was not selfishly used, arguing that,

38. Little, *Religious Poverty and the Profit Economy in Medieval Europe*, 216.

39. Langholm, *Economics in the Medieval Schools*, 564.

40. Ibid., 594.

41. Tawney, *Religion and the Rise of Capitalism*, 73.

42. Wood, *Medieval Economic Thought*, 18.

since the Fall, property needed to be protected from the avarice of sinful human nature. Aquinas went further. He recognized that community of goods would seem to be in accordance with natural law. At the same time, however, he recognized the value of "positive" (i.e., human) law as a supplement to natural law, and that human agreement seems to realize private property to be necessary for the common good. He himself justifies this with three utilitarian arguments: (1) "Every man is more careful to procure [or look after] what is for himself alone"; (2) "Human affairs are conducted in a more orderly fashion"; and (3) "A more peaceful state is ensured."[43]

Meanwhile, great legal changes were taking place with regard to the holding of property. Throughout the feudal period, the theory was that no land was privately owned. The lord had "dominion" over it, but, unless he was the king, he himself was a tenant. There is much disagreement as to the origins of English Common Law, but at some time in this period it became possible for free tenants to appeal to the king's courts to claim possession of land based on inheritance. At the same time, in the newly developing towns, it became possible to claim ownership of a particular property.[44] The judgments of the scholastics can be understood, in general terms, as in support of these changes. In relation to the question of private property, however, the door was being opened to an acceptance of the old Roman Law of absolute private ownership, and so to an acceptance of an unequal ownership.

In practice, the courts increasingly defended absolute ownership.[45] Its philosophical justification can be found in the works of writers like Hobbes and Locke, deducing their arguments from what they perceived in nature. Most significantly for us, Locke states his conviction on many occasions that the central function of government is the protection of property: "The great and chief end therefore of men uniting into Commonwealth, and putting themselves under Government, is the preservation of their property."[46] And, in defining property, he says, "Whatsoever [a man] removes from the state that Nature hath provided, and left it in, he hath mixed his labor with, and joined it to something that is his own,

43. Aquinas, *Summa Theologica*, part II, 2nd part, q, 66, art. 2, p. 224.

44. Wood, *Medieval Economic Thought*, 33–36.

45. Duchrow and Hinkelammert, *Property for People, Not for Profit*, 33.

46. Locke, *Second Treatise of Government*, 9.124.

and thereby makes it his property."[47] This applies particularly to land.[48] This appropriation of land can continue as long as there is enough left for others to do the same,[49] provided it is worked on by his own labor,[50] and provided that no one possesses more than he can make use of.[51]

Locke realizes, however, that difficulties begin to arise when land becomes scarce, so that communities have to establish the limits of each person's land[52]—and as soon as there is a monetary system, in that this enables people to acquire more than their labor has worked on. Locke concludes, "It is plain that men have agreed to disproportionate and unequal possession of the earth, they having by tacit and voluntary consent found out a way, how a man may fairly possess more land than he himself can use the product of, by receiving in exchange for the overplus gold and silver, which may be hoarded up without injury to anyone, these metals not spoiling or decaying in the hands of the possessor."[53] In this new situation (he claims) the individual voluntarily surrenders his natural right to defend his property to the state; the state, by establishing and enforcing laws, then serves as a kind of umpire in disputes that may arise.

It is surely an extravagant claim that poor people have voluntarily consented to the creation of their own poverty. A key word in Locke's argument, however, is the word "tacit." No human being would consent with understanding to such an arrangement. But it seems to me that Locke—almost without realizing it—has here unearthed one of the great problems with money—that is, the fact that the use of money inevitably (whether you realize it or not) produces inequality, unless steps are taken to counteract it. This produces one of the important reasons for regulating markets, as the scholastics realized. Hobbes, to his credit, appreciated this to some degree, and proposed his strong sovereign power to prevent the struggle of capital and labor from getting violent. To his discredit, however, he did not actually believe in regulating markets, reckoning the market price for everything to be the correct price. In this way he removed any sense of justice from monetary affairs. In the case of

47. Ibid., 5.27.
48. Ibid., 5.32.
49. Ibid., 5.36.
50. Ibid., 5.36.
51. Ibid., 5.40.
52. Ibid., 5.45.
53. Ibid., 5.50.

Locke, the state is established by the people with the particular purpose of protecting the private property that is considered to generate wealth for everybody (though especially, of course, for the owners of capital). Again, however, this is not on the basis of any kind of justice.

Justice and the Common Good

Since Locke, the global economy has been built on the foundation that he justified. For much of this time the dominant philosophy has been that of laissez faire, letting the market price be the judge in all transactions. Particularly in Roman Catholic theology, however, there have always been those who were convinced that moral considerations must prevail, and this point was strongly made by Leo XIII in his famous encyclical *Rerum Novarum* (1891), usually regarded as the first papal encyclical on economic matters. Theologically, the encyclical is based on the validity of natural law, to which Leo had recommitted the church in 1879 in his encyclical *Aeterni Patris*, and to which all aspects of life, including the economic, were supposed to be subject.[54] In particular, Leo laid strong emphasis on justice as the crucial criterion by which issues should be judged—and justice was held to require that the common good of the whole community must take preference over individual gain.

The encyclical begins with a clear recognition of the plight of working people in the industrial era. "There can be no question whatever that some remedy must be found, and quickly found, for the misery and wretchedness which press so heavily at this moment on the large majority of the very poor." And very quickly, Leo locates what he sees as a major source of the problem: that "working men have been given over, isolated and defenceless, to the callousness of employers and the greed of unrestrained competition." Of particular interest in the context of our argument, he goes on: "The evil has been increased by rapacious usury, which, although more than once condemned by the church, is nevertheless, under a different form but with the same guilt, still practised by avaricious

---

54. This same encyclical also returned the church to a particular appreciation of the work of Thomas Aquinas. It may be found printed as an introduction to the *Summa Theologica* (English translation, 1920).

and grasping men." The eventual result has been "to lay upon the masses of the poor a yoke little better than slavery itself."[55]

Already at this point, therefore, we see the opposition of the pope to unbridled capitalism and laissez-faire economics, under which money is allowed free rein. The reference to usury is quite surprising, considering the fact that the principle of charging interest had been accepted for many years. What is clearly being referred to is the charging of excessive interest. Unfortunately, this is not a subject to which Leo returns, except insofar as he urges employers to treat their employees on the basis of justice rather than seeking the maximum profits for themselves. It does reveal, nevertheless, a deep suspicion of the capitalist system that was to survive for many years (as it did in the Church of England). The revival also of the idea of a just wage and the encouragement of various activities on the part of the state are clear indications that the philosophy of laissez faire was regarded as totally inadequate for the situation being faced.

At the same time it has to be recognized that the pope totally opposed what he calls "socialism" (or communism), the prime evil of which he sees as the confiscation of private property. Right at the beginning, he says of the socialists, "their proposals are so clearly futile for all practical purposes, that if they were carried out the working man himself would be among the first to suffer. Moreover they are emphatically unjust, because they would rob the lawful possessor, bring the state into a sphere that is not its own, and cause complete confusion in the community."[56] Strangely enough, though Leo contends that private property is in accordance with natural law, he produces an argument for this which appears to come from Locke as much as from the Catholic natural law tradition: "When man spends the industry of his mind and the strength of his body in procuring the fruits of nature, by that act he makes his own that portion of nature's field which he cultivates."[57] Thomas Aquinas (following Aristotle) had held that *community* of goods was part of the natural law, private property being expedient because of the covetousness of other human beings. In the sixteenth and seventeenth centuries, however, the church had come to accept the assumption among property owners that they had

---

55. *Rerum Novarum*, para. 2; translation in O'Brien and Shannon, *Catholic Social Thought*.

56. Ibid., para. 3.

57. Ibid., para. 7.

an absolute right to their property (as in the Roman law tradition), and scholars like Grotius had turned this into a natural right.[58]

Though allowing a significant role for the state, Leo opposes too much state intervention in the economy. He says, "True, if a family finds itself in great difficulty, utterly friendless, and without prospect of help, it is right that extreme necessity be met by public aid. . . . But the rulers of the State must go no further: nature bids them stop here."[59] What he feels to be the correct way of helping the poor is (a) private charity, (b) Workmen's Associations—by which he means any institution created voluntarily for the help of the needy—not particularly a trade union (though there does appear to be scope for these, provided that their purposes are not "evidently bad, unjust or dangerous to the State").[60] It is obvious that his chief complaint at this point is the way that the property of Catholic charitable organizations was being confiscated[61]—when, in his view, these organizations were the best way of ministering to the poor.

While Leo holds back at certain points, what cannot be doubted is that the whole encyclical is dominated by a great suspicion of laissez-faire economics and of an unrestrained seeking after profits, together with a desire that other motivations have a dominant role in economic affairs. Here we encounter reference to "the common good"[62] and "justice for all,"[63] and the whole encyclical ends with a great paean in praise of love.[64] Here also is a section on the right use of money, which strongly makes the point that, even if it is lawful to hold private property, "man should not consider his outward possessions as his own, but as common to all, so as to share them without difficulty when others are in need."[65] In words like

---

58. Duchrow and Hinkelammert, *Property for People, Not for Profit*, 33–34.

59. *Rerum Novarum*, para. 11.

60. Ibid., para. 38.

61. Ibid., para. 39.

62. "It is the province of the commonwealth to consult for the common good" (Ibid., para. 26).

63. "Among the many and grave duties of rulers who want to do the best for their people, the first and chief is to act with strict justice—with that justice which is called in the schools "distributive"—towards each and every class" (Ibid., para. 27).

64. "The happy results we all long for must be chiefly brought about by the plenteous outpouring of charity" (Ibid., para. 45).

65. Ibid., para. 19.

this, the problem of inequality is clearly recognized, together with the need to take action about it.

The whole subject is taken further in Catholic teaching with the development in the mid-twentieth century of the idea of fundamental human rights, not least through the thinking of Jacques Maritain.[66] The idea of fundamental human rights is tackled at length in Pope John XXIII's encyclical *Pacem in Terris* (1963), where the first of such rights is stated as "the right to life and a worthy standard of living," in which each person has "the right to security in the case of . . . any [situation] in which he is deprived of the means of subsistence through no fault of his own."[67] The "preferential option for the poor" is given its first encyclical mention in that same document: "Consideration of justice and equity . . . can at times demand that those in civil government give more attention to the less fortunate members of the community, since they are less able to defend their rights and to assert their legitimate claims."[68] Since that time, justice and the common good have continued to be the major themes in Catholic social teaching—so that, in his encyclical *Caritas in Veritate* (2009), Pope Benedict XVI (known generally as a conservative pope) can say, "Justice is the primary way of charity . . . an integral part of love 'in deed and in truth' (1 John 3.18), to which Saint John exhorts us. . . . Charity demands justice: recognition and respect for the legitimate rights of individuals and peoples."[69] Similarly, "To desire the *common good* and strive towards it is *a requirement of justice and charity.*"[70]

In specific relation to economic matters, Benedict says:

> The world's wealth is growing in absolute terms, but inequalities are on the increase. . . .
>
> the *primary capital to be safeguarded and valued is man, the human person in his or her integrity.* . . .
>
> the conviction that the economy must be autonomous, that it must be shielded from "influences" of a moral character, has led men to abuse the economic process in a thoroughly destructive way. . . .

---

66. Stiltner, *Religion and the Common Good*, ch. 3.

67. John XXIII, *Pacem in Terris*, para. 11.

68. Ibid., para. 56.

69. Benedict XVI, *Caritas in Veritate*, para. 6.

70. Ibid., para. 7.

the social doctrine of the Church has unceasingly highlighted the importance of *distributive justice* and *social justice for the market economy*. . . .

the entire financial system has to be aimed at sustaining true development.[71]

How this is to be done, however, we are not told—beyond the need for financiers to "rediscover the genuinely ethical foundation of their activity . . . the regulation of the financial sector, so as to safeguard weaker parties and discourage scandalous speculation," and "experimentation with new forms of finance, designed to support development projects." As in the past, what seems to be missing is any clear appreciation in the encyclical of how radical a solution is actually required to deal with the power of money in the capitalist system, or that the system is fatally flawed. Unfortunately, he passes quickly over the question of the market, suggesting that the problem is not with the market in itself so much as in what people make it. This paragraph is carefully nuanced, and contains some important recognitions, for instance, "The market does not exist in the pure state. It is shaped by the cultural configurations which define it and give it direction," and "The market can be a negative force, not because it is so by nature, but because a certain ideology [laissez faire?] can make it so." At the same time, his emphasis is on what people do with the market: "Instruments that are good in themselves can be transformed into harmful ones. But it is man's darkened reason that produces these consequences, not the instrument *per se*. Therefore *it is not the instrument that must be called to account, but individuals* (my italics), their moral conscience and their personal and social responsibility."[72]

A similar criticism could be made of the document commissioned by the Vatican specifically to deal with the ethical issues raised by the vast increase in financial activity since the 1970s.[73] This document makes a noble attempt to tackle some of the ethical issues involved, concluding with advice to individuals, financiers, company managers, and public authorities about the ethical attitudes they should take, but it fails completely to consider the question of the nature of money and how it should be evaluated. This failure is noted by Catherine Cowley in her book *The*

71. Ibid., paras. 23, 25, 34, 35, 65.
72. Ibid., para. 36.
73. de Salins and de Galhan, *The Modern Development of Financial Activities*.

Value of Money: Ethics and the World of Finance, where she observes that, since the decline of scholasticism, this has been a subject generally neglected by Catholic writers: "As the understanding of the nature of money and the relationship between money and time changed, the [scholastic] teaching [on the nature of money] was first adapted and then finally dropped. Although reflection on economic matters continued, it did so without developing a new understanding of money to replace the one left behind."[74]

Despite this lack, it would not be right to downplay the enormous significance of the theology of the common good and its criticism of dangers produced by the dominance of money. Particularly since 1989, when Herman Daly and John Cobb Jr. produced their manifesto for "redirecting the economy toward community, the environment, and a sustainable future" (the subtitle for their book *The Common Good*), the concept of the common good has become widely accepted currency in thinking aimed at overcoming the inequalities apparent in the global economy.[75]

Justice and Christian Socialism

It was the suffering produced by the Industrial Revolution that produced in Britain the movement of Christian Socialism, following the lead of F. D. Maurice (1805–1872), who published a seminal work in 1838 entitled *The Kingdom of Christ or Letters to a Quaker concerning the Principles, Conceptions and Ordinances of the Catholic Church*, in which his primary assertion was that Christ had not come to establish a religious sect or a new society but a kingdom.[76] It was God's will that this kingdom should embrace all people, rich and poor, and that the whole world should be brought under the rule of Christ. In the words of John Atherton, this "reflected a fundamentally important transformation in church life, and therefore in society, from stressing the atonement to focussing on the incarnation."[77] In the thinking of Maurice, every human being was in Christ, part of one body, and, instead of engaging in competition with

74. Cowley, *The Value of Money*, 93–94.

75. As in June O'Connor, "Making a Case for the Common Good in a Global Economy—the United Nations Human Development Reports (1990–2001)."

76. Maurice, *The Kingdom of Christ*.

77. Atherton, *Christianity and the Market*, 141.

each other, they should be working together for the good of all. "Christ came to establish a kingdom, not to proclaim a set of opinions. Every man entering this kingdom becomes interested in all its relations, members, circumstances; he cannot separate himself in anywise from them; he cannot establish a life or interest apart from theirs."[78]

Up till then, Anglicans had always been suspicious of radical proposals for social change, not least those of the Chartists, because they had often been anticlerical. Maurice was not a revolutionary, but aimed to strike at the roots of the prevailing system of competition by encouraging worker cooperatives, where people could work together, sharing the profits. He also realized that, in order to manage their own affairs, working people needed more opportunities for education, and this led to the foundation of the Working Men's College, of which he became the first principal. He worked with a small group of fellow enthusiasts, not least John Ludlow (1821–1911) and Charles Kingsley (1819–1875). Together they produced a series of pamphlets entitled "Politics of the People," a series that only lasted a few months, but created a great impression. The name "Christian Socialists," which they chose for themselves, was meant to be provocative, underlining their conviction that Christianity stood for a society in which people worked together rather than in competition.

The first phase of the movement may be said to have come to an end in 1854, when Maurice closed his Society for Promoting Working Men's Associations, but the next twenty years did see the growth of incarnational theology throughout the church. In 1877 a new generation of clergy organized themselves in the Guild of St. Matthew. Its founder, Stewart Headlam (1847–1924), pursued a more radical and political course than the earlier group. His was a socialism committed to the redistribution of wealth, the reform of land, and secular education for all. He was particularly attracted by the Single Tax of the American, Henry George, who advocated the taxation of land as the way to produce a just society. Another organization, founded in 1889, was the Christian Social Union (CSU), which was more academic and had a larger membership.

The CSU was a formidable institution in its time. For instance, at the end of the century, about two-thirds of all Oxford undergraduates belonged to it,[79] and in the period 1889–1913, fourteen out of the fifty-

---

78. Maurice, *The Kingdom of Christ*, 3:387.
79. Waterman, *Political Economy and Christian Theology*, 214.

three bishops appointed were CSU members.[80] As the twentieth century continued, most pronouncements of the Church of England on social issues reflected this standpoint. That is not to say that there was unanimity among those who belonged to this tradition. There was, in fact, considerable variety in understanding of the word *socialist*. For some it meant little more than cooperative activity.[81] At the other extreme were those who sought the nationalization of banks and the major means of production.[82] The CSU tended to have a very broad membership. The Guild of St. Matthew (until its demise 1909) was further to the left, as was the Church Socialist League (formed in 1906). This was split in 1923 into the Anglo-Catholic League of the Kingdom of God (which avoided all references to socialism or common ownership) and the Society of Socialist Christians, which was interdenominational and affiliated with the Labour Party.[83]

The way it turned out was that writers in this tradition either spoke generally of the need for a change in the economic system or else advocated reforms aimed at dealing with what were felt to be its most damaging features. Examples are "the living [minimum] wage" (first proposed in church circles in the Canterbury Convocation report, *The Moral Witness of the Church on Economic Subjects*; 1907),[84] nationalization (advocated by William Temple at the Pan-Anglican Congress of 1908),[85] taxes on land (as included in the 1909 budget),[86] and increases in death duties (in the publication *Competition* produced by the Collegium group in 1916).[87] Many of these proposals were included in the *Fifth Report* (1919) produced by one of the Archbishops' Committees of Inquiry following the National Mission of 1916, and in the reports of the Conference on Christian Politics, Economics and Citizenship (COPEC) of 1924.

---

80. Atherton, *Christianity and the Market*, 181.

81. "Socialism is the opposite of Individualism, and it is by contrast with Individualism that the true character of Socialism can be discerned" (Official Report of the Church Congress held at Hull. London, 1890), 320.

82. "Churchmen can unite with Socialists of every sort in their endeavour to seize the state and use it for the well-being of the masses instead of the classes" (Headlam, *Christian Socialism*, 6).

83. Wilkinson, *Christian Socialism*, 143–44.

84. Ibid., 91.

85. Ibid., 58.

86. Ibid., 59.

87. Norman, *Church and Society in England, 1770–1970*, 241.

The outstanding figure in this tradition was undoubtedly William Temple, who was Archbishop of Canterbury from 1942 to 1944. Right from the beginning of his ministry, Temple was outspoken on social and economic issues. In 1909 he formed the Collegium group whose chief production was the volume *Competition* (produced in 1913 but not published till 1916). He joined the Labour Party in 1918, but withdrew on his appointment to Manchester (so, he said, that the church should not be seen to have any party political bias). At Manchester, York, and Canterbury, he continued to speak out, and played major roles in the COPEC, Oxford, and Malvern conferences devoted to social issues. Robert Craig is right to point out, however, as others have also done, that "after 1924 [COPEC] Temple came to see the manifest inadequacy of his ethico-social approach to the human situation. For example, he came to see that his call to self-sacrifice and his neglect of the principle of concrete justice had been a grievous error. . . . Temple saw the Christian in society called to think in terms of justice as well as love, of rights as well as duties. This increasing realism [fired, we may say, by his contacts with Reinhold Niebuhr] marks his latter years."[88]

Edward Norman is right to say that probably the greatest contribution to the social Christianity that Temple had done so much to foster was his Penguin Special, *Christianity and the Social Order*, published in 1942, just before his translation to Canterbury.[89] The significance of this book was chiefly that it was brief and widely read, and that it revealed to the general public the extent to which socialist values had reached the highest levels of the church.[90] Temple was careful to say that the church as an institution should not advocate any particular policy in the political and economic realm, but confine itself to general principles.[91] He also emphasized that he was not simply advocating socialism. "The question is . . . How Socialist and how individualist shall we be?"[92] He went on, however, in an appendix, to state his own views on many of the practical issues of the time—views that were strongly socialist in their emphasis. He talked, for instance, about the nationalization of commercial banks,

88. Craig, *Social Concern in the Thought of William Temple*, 123–24.

89. Norman, *Church and Society in England, 1770–1970*, 367.

90. It was advertised on its front cover as "A statement of the beliefs of the People's Archbishop that all secular policy should be founded upon Christian truth."

91. Temple, *Christianity and the Social Order*, 28.

92. Ibid., 102.

the nationalization of urban land, and the participation of workers on the boards of the companies for which they worked. He even mentioned the radical idea that he called "withering capital"—according to which, as soon as the interest paid on any investment is equal to the sum invested, the principal should be reduced by a specific amount each year until the claim of the investor to interest or dividends is extinguished.[93]

Temple's methodology (in the main part of the book) relied heavily on what he called "Natural Law," following the emphasis of the Christendom group, rather than on appeal to the Scriptures (though he did lay much emphasis on the doctrine of the human being made in the image of God, revealed in the Scriptures). The conclusions he drew, however, reveal the difficulty of deducing moral prescriptions from natural law, unless they are to consist of vague generalities. He finished up, therefore, with some very general statements, such as, "The aim of a Christian social order is the fullest possible development of individual personality in the widest and deepest possible fellowship."[94] And, in relation to capitalism, he said, "For economic production there *must* be profits, there *ought* to be regard for the consumer's interest, and it is wrong to sacrifice that interest to the increase of profits above a reasonable figure. . . . Industry, commerce etc is to be judged by its success in promoting or facilitating the true ends of human life—religion, art, science, and, above all, happy relationships."[95] In the appendix, as already noted, he did produce more detailed proposals (his own, rather than church's), but clearly felt these could not be deduced directly from natural law.

What is remarkable is that Temple not only absorbed these views but also advocated them publicly at every opportunity, despite the fact that his knowledge of economics was limited and that he was bound to be attacked by the economics profession.[96] Not surprisingly perhaps, his opinions aroused considerable controversy. Could an Archbishop of Canterbury express personal opinions in public? Did he know enough about economics to speak publicly on such issues? The general response, however, was enthusiastic and favorable, not necessarily because everybody accepted his arguments, but because the leader of the church had had the

93. Ibid., 111.

94. Ibid., 100.

95. Ibid., 82.

96. Temple, *The Church Looks Forward*, 116–17.

courage to speak out on issues at the core of national life.[97] Many have felt his detailed prescriptions to be basically impractical. Certainly, with his death, the end of the war and the new political situation that followed, such ideas were less prominently expressed. To some extent, however, this was due to the fact that the legislation of the new Labour government put into law so much of what people like Temple had been seeking. It would not be too much to claim that the achievements of the post-war Labour government can be attributed to a great degree to the long campaign waged by Christian Socialists over more than fifty years.

Prophets are not always gifted in the detailed government of society, but Temple's prophetic role (in particular) in seeking to make a Christian voice heard in economic and political affairs had been of enormous significance. From our point of view, what Temple represents is a remarkable example of a theologian who was deeply aware of the dangers involved in allowing unrestrained use of money. It is not so clear whether he appreciated consciously that money is a problem *in itself*. What is significant, however, is that he was prepared in his later years to use his position in order to challenge the very basis of the capitalist economic system on theological grounds. What is to be regretted is that, in the post-war years, this challenge gradually faded.

Capitalism under Fire

After the thirty-year post-war honeymoon, the mid-1970s witnessed the breakdown of many of the certainties bred by the Enlightenment movement. It could be said that the two world wars dealt its deathblow, but that it actually took thirty years to die. The reverberations of this sea change can be seen in theologies like Liberation Theology (which we shall discuss later), the Political Theology associated particularly with Jürgen Moltmann, the Neo-Barthianism of Stanley Hauerwas, and the Radical Orthodoxy associated particularly with John Milbank.

Faith in the City (the Report of the Archbishop of Canterbury's Commission on Urban Priority Areas) was probably the most influential Church of England report since *Towards the Conversion of England* (1944). It achieved popular fame because it was seen to oppose the conservative policies of Baroness Thatcher's government, in power at the

97. Iremonger, *William Temple*, 581.

time. The report talks, for instance, of "grave and fundamental injustice in the UPAs [Urban Priority Areas]. . . . No adequate response is being made by government, nation or church."[98] It also calls on Christians to beware of slogans like "the creation of wealth" (3.13) and "industry must be more efficient" (3.14), which tend to establish themselves as self-evident maxims.

> It is a clear duty for the Church to sound a warning that society may be losing the compassionate character which is still desired by the majority of its members (3.18). . . . It is unrealistic to assume that even the skilled and mobile residents of our cities can all 'get on their bikes' [Lord Tebbit's phrase] and move (9.30). . . . Some may argue that the benefits of economic growth will somhow "trickle down" to unemployed people in the UPAs. We are not convinced by such arguments (9.32). . . . Recent history has, on the contrary, seen an increasing divide between rich and poor (9.33). . . . We believe that at present too much emphasis is being given to individualism, and not enough to collective obligation. (9.46)

From the point of view of this book, most significant in the report is, undoubtedly, the concerted opposition of the report to the neoliberal economic thinking of the Conservative government. No commission member entered a minority report. On the contrary, the commission goes out of its way to say, "*We are united* in the view that the costs of present policies, with the continuing growth of unemployment, are unacceptable in their effect on whole communities and generations" (9.50, italics mine). It could be argued, perhaps, that the report was produced at a time when this reflected a widely held opinion in society, and such unanimity might not have been achieved in different circumstances. The commission does appear to reflect, however, the kind of theology that was beginning to take over from the classical liberal approach. In a significant passage, they write,

> There is no generally agreed manifesto for a Christian social order. Yet this long tradition of Christian social thinking, if it does not offer an immediate alternative to the present economic and political system, has nevertheless kept alive the fundamental Christian conviction that even in this fallen world there are possibilities for a better ordering of society. (3.13)

---

98. *Faith in the City*, xv. References for the quotations that follow are given in the text and cite paragraphs.

And "These challenges addressed to widely accepted maxims arise not from a clearly defined Christian social and political philosophy but from the existence in Scripture of a different paradigm of social and economic relationships" (3.16). On this basis, the commission does feel able to speak confidently on a broad range of practical issues. What is missing, perhaps, is any explicit statement that the weakness of the neoliberal position might stem from its reliance on the unfettered use of money.

A fully fledged Christian attack on capitalism finally arrived in Timothy Gorringe's *Capital and the Kingdom* (1994), with its penetrating account of the phenomenon of capitalism, and its blow-by-blow description of the devastating effects of the free economy on human life and the cosmos. Gorringe traces the origins of this situation to the separation between ethics and economics that became established during the Enlightenment, and describes his aim as an attempt to bring them together again in an understanding of the significance of the kingdom of God. He highlights the particular role of prophecy that is a voice from outside the system of prevailing morality, calling humanity back to values that sustain community and fullness of life for all.

The economic system, he says, is not a self-evident system of iron laws to be unquestioningly obeyed, but one that has been created and manipulated by those with power in order to suit their own ends. Of the gods worshipped in this system, which now envelops the world, he identifies growth (p. 80), efficiency (p. 85), competition (p. 98), private property (p. 115), and individualism (p. 121). Those who have suffered most, he says, have been the inhabitants of underdeveloped countries, and the most devastating factor in that has been debt. "The reason for this fiasco, perhaps better described as wickedness, is the compulsion to put growth and profit (which involves lifestyle) before everything else. . . . the net effect of giving absolute priority to profit is death."[99] According to Gorringe, at least three fundamental considerations demand church pressure for a different economic order: (1) Its control has to be changed. (2) Debts have to be remitted. (3) Priority has to be given to that which produces life.[100]

The final chapter then identifies two ways that can be followed (echoing Deuteronomy 30:19)—that which leads to death, and that which leads to life. It is not too late, he says, for the human race to choose life

99. Gorringe, *Capital and the Kingdom*, 139.
100. Ibid., 140–41.

(though the ecological clock is steadily running down)—and, from the point of view of my thesis, it is significant that he finds a crucial place for a total renewal of the role of money. "The money system could be *redeemed* through a recognition of the proper function of money as enabling people to transact with one another and act conservingly [instead of being a means of profit]."[101] The end of it all would be to produce a system in which the resources of the world are used not for the benefit of the few, but to produce a prosperous, just, and secure future for all.

Another strong critique of capitalism is David Jenkins's book *Market Whys and Wherefores* (2000). Through his work at William Temple College, and later at Durham, and through his personal involvement in the trauma of the Miners' Strike, Jenkins had come face to face with the corrosive effects of an unbridled economy, and his aim throughout the book is to challenge the free market fundamentalism that insists There Is No Alternative to it (TINA). In the opening chapter he describes his realization that "the Market is increasingly run by money for money."[102] In saying this, however, I do not think he is talking about money as such. Rather he is saying that the Market is run by those with money, for the benefit of those with money. In other words, that money is a *tool* used by those who are rich to enable them to become richer. Surprisingly, despite all his railing against the free market, he never rails against money. Without ever saying so, it is almost as though he regards money as a *neutral* element in the economy, neither good nor evil—what is wrong (as many others hold) is the way that it is *used*. On the other hand, such a devastating attack on the free market as he makes in this book could be interpreted (as I would wish to do) as an acknowledgment of the harm that money does *when left to itself*. He certainly recognizes that money is a critical element in the functioning of the free market. "Its very nature, which operates by money, means that it is less and less likely to respond to messages about real and basic needs. The only individuals who count in a trading transaction model are those with access to money. It is only through money that they can register, even remotely, effective messages as far as the Market is concerned."[103] In addition, if the free market (as he says) is an idol, then it is not a great step to treating uncontrolled money as also an idol.

101. Ibid., 167.

102. Jenkins, *Market Whys and Human Wherefores*, 4.

103. Ibid., 120.

Conclusions

It is only fair to point out that there have also been examples of Christian writers who have supported the free market system, for all its problems, as the best way of allocating limited resources, encouraging entrepreneurial enterprise, and so forth.[104] Tracking Christian theology across the centuries, however, it is not difficult to see that, for much of the time, there has been great suspicion of any economic system where money has been given free rein. And the chief objection has been to the injustice and inequality it always produces, opening up a division between those with too little money and those with too much.

For most of history, governments concerned about this inequality have had to resort to regulations of various kinds in order to restrict injustice, and theologians have encouraged them in it. What this has often done, however, is to obscure the fundamental problem that, wherever money is used, inequalities will inevitably follow. Even Wilkinson and Pickett, in their otherwise brilliant exposé of the phenomenon of inequality, only hint that the root of the problem could be in the use of money, when they say, "it is hard to escape the conclusion that the high levels [of inequality] in our societies reflect the concentrations of power in our economic institutions"[105]—referring to the stranglehold of governments by a few mammoth companies.

Since the deregulation of the seventies, the problem has been, for those with eyes to see, much more evident than it was before. The crisis that began in 2007 has made it even clearer, so that even academic economists have begun to raise the possibility that the capitalist system needs a fundamental re-formation. The emphasis of this chapter has been to show the consistent recognition by Christian writers of the injustice that is always produced by unrestricted use of money, and to argue that this can only be corrected by radical reform based on a quest for justice.

104. Notable Christian advocates of this position in recent years have been Michael Novak (Catholic, USA) and Brian Griffiths (Church of England).

105. Wilkinson and Pickett, *The Spirit Level*, 249.

Money and Value

IN THE LAST THREE chapters I have been dealing primarily with money as a means of exchange and the degree to which money is a satisfactory means of exchange. One of the basic points made in all textbooks about money, however, is that, as well as being a means of exchange, it is also a measure of value and a store of value. Such an obvious statement may seem to need little discussion, but the question remains of how adequately money performs this function; the purpose of this chapter is to assess that question from the point of view of Christian theology.

When we talk about the "value" of anything, we are talking about how much it means to us, and this talk implies that some things mean more to us than others. The big question, however, is in what way value is to be measured. Is it a subjective matter, to be measured by the strength of our feelings? Or is there any objective way in which it can be done? Despite the increasing pressure being exerted in the present capitalist economy, one thing about which Christians have been adamant is that valuation does not have to be in terms of money. Many of the things we value most—like good relationships, happiness, and peace of mind—certainly cannot be valued in such terms.

The same sort of thing can be said of the "values" that form the subject of so much ethical discussion today. Alasdair MacIntyre has described the collapse of the language of virtues in the face of the increasing secularization of society. In its place we now have discussion of the values accepted by individuals, groups, or traditions—the moral evaluations that lie at the heart of a worldview or culture, which produce our practical actions. In a pluralist society these values will vary considerably. To understand them is to understand the roots of most of the conflicts in the world. What is certain is that they cannot be expressed in terms of money.

At this point, therefore, it is helpful to identify (as many writers do) values inherent in the Christian tradition that are constituent of ethical behavior, which may often differ from those of other traditions and those prevalent in particular societies. In the Old Testament Torah, one could distinguish especially the values of solidarity, mercy, and justice, and in the New Testament, those of self-sacrificial love and service. The Sermon on the Mount, in particular, is often described as a manifesto for the kingdom of God, which enshrines values that were (and still are) distinctly countercultural. Similarly, in the early church Fathers one can identify the particular values of sharing and generosity. The importance of this, from our point of view, is that such values are impossible to state in money terms, and they will often lead to courses of action strikingly different from those based on monetary valuations. It will be the contention of this chapter that there is a radical inconsistency between the values inherent in the Christian tradition and any system where values are primarily measured in terms of money. I shall look particularly at the contribution of Philip Goodchild.

Difficulties in Measuring Value

As already indicated, the major concern of the Christian scholastics in the realm of economics was to consider the factors involved in establishing a "just" price for any item—treating the whole matter as a moral issue. It was one thing, however, to regard this as a moral issue, and another thing altogether to work out how such a price should be reached. For many writers, the just price was simply the current market price. This would be produced by the factors of demand and supply. Some reckoned that prices (especially wages) might sometimes need to be fixed by public authority. What was universally condemned was the creation of monopolies, since these would allow the powerful to take advantage of the weak and the poor. Altogether, despite difficulties of calculation, the scholastics were convinced that, somehow, there was a price that was (morally) right.

Adam Smith argued that there are, in fact, two values for anything—a "real" or "natural" value, and a "nominal" or "market" value. The "real" price of anything, to Smith, is the toil and trouble of acquiring it, of which the chief element is the cost of labor. On the other hand, Smith recognized that "though labour be the real measure of the exchangeable value of all commodities, it is not that by which their value is commonly estimated," but "it is adjusted . . . by the 'haggling and bargaining of the market.'"[1] He settled, however, for the idea that "labour . . . is the only universal as well as the only accurate measure of value."[2] He eventually concluded, "When the price of any commodity is neither more nor less than what is sufficient to pay the rent of the land, the wages of the labour, and the profits of the stock employed in raising, preparing, and bringing it to market, according to their natural rates, the commodity is then sold for what may be called its natural price."[3] The "market" price, however, "is regulated by the proportion between the quantity which is actually brought to market, and the demand of those who are willing to pay the natural price of the commodity."[4] Significantly, perhaps, Smith merely described this distinction without making any judgments on it.

In a similar vein, Karl Marx made his distinction between "use value" and "exchange value."[5] Like Smith, Marx placed great store on the labor involved in production and distribution, and described use value as having value "because abstract human labour is objectified or materialized in it."[6] The same is true of exchange value. The difference, however, is that it is always exchange value that we meet in market exchanges. "If commodities could speak, they would say this: our use value may interest men, but it does not belong to us as objects. What does belong to us as objects, however, is our value. Our own intercourse as commodities proves it. We relate to each other merely as exchange values."[7] And these, Marx said, have come to be expressed in terms of another commodity, the universal equivalent (i.e., money).[8]

As with Smith, Marx was restricted by his identification of money with a physical commodity. He, therefore, had to say, "As measure of value, and as standard of price, money performs two quite different functions. It is the measure of value as the social incarnation of human labour; it is the standard of price as a quantity of metal with a fixed weight"[9] (so that

1. Smith, *Wealth of Nations*, 134.
2. Ibid., 139–40.
3. Ibid., 158.
4. Ibid.
5. Marx, *Capital*, bk. 1, ch. 1, p. 126.
6. Ibid., p. 129.
7. Ibid., pp. 176–77.
8. Ibid., ch. 2, p. 180.
9. Ibid., ch. 3, p. 192.

he had to make allowances for the fact that the value of this metal may vary from time to time). He also had (for us) what is sometimes called a "transformation problem," in that he was never able to explain exactly how particular amounts of labor congeal into a particular price. This is the weakness of any labor theory of value. But this did not seem to trouble him. He was far more interested in his conviction that the money value that emerges from transactions symbolizes the social relations involved in production and distribution (not least the relations between labor and capital)—to which I shall turn in a later chapter.

Money as the Measure of All Value

This leads on to what has concerned philosophers, sociologists, and theologians since that time—namely, the way in which money value has increasingly come to displace all other measures of value. So Georg Simmel (in 1912), describing money as the perfect example of a tool (in that it exists purely for the purpose of exchange) and a means to an end (the accomplishment of exchanges), describes it also as "the most extreme example of a means becoming an end."[10] As such (as we shall see in the next chapter) it becomes the supreme object of desire, and "possesses a significant relationship to the notion of a god—a relationship that only psychology, which has the privilege of being unable to commit blasphemy [!], may disclose."[11] Simmel also underlines something that has been increasingly realized since: that "one of the major tendencies of life—the reduction of quality to quantity—achieves its highest and uniquely perfect representation in money."[12]

In recent years, this reduction has been recognized by a number of writers. Craig Gay, in his appropriately titled *Cash Values*, says,

> I want to argue that our pervasive use of, and increasing reliance upon, the tool we call "money"—the very tool that capitalism has put to such good use—has indeed subtly altered our interests and the things we think about. It has also subtly altered our symbols and the things we think with. Finally, it has subtly altered our communities and the forums in which our thoughts develop.[13]

10. Simmel, *The Philosophy of Money*, 232.
11. Ibid., 236.
12. Ibid., 280.
13. Gay, *Cash Values*, 59.

"Money Metric's relentless reduction of quality to quantity . . . hollows out our entire world view, depriving us of any sense that life is inherently meaningful and that it has been endowed with qualities that far transcend monetary valuation."[14] Nick Spencer, in another appropriately titled book, *The Measure of All Things?* (2003), lists a number of particular problems that this orientation produces: first (as we have already seen) many of the things that actually make us happy cannot be bought with money;[15] second, when money becomes the yardstick for value, all other measures are invariably displaced, and anything that doesn't make money is regarded as of questionable worth.[16] This he illustrates in relation to the unprecedented encroaching of commercial interests on public space,[17] the danger of political decisions being made on the basis of money,[18] and the normal tendency of consumers to purchase items on the basis of price rather than quality or the principles behind their manufacture.[19]

In line with the particular emphasis of the Jubilee Centre, however, Spencer reckons that the most corrosive effect of valuing everything in terms of money is on our relationships with one another, in that relationships come to be based on financial criteria—resulting in the contractualization of relationships and the litigation culture. Indeed the individual person can even come to be evaluated according to how much money one has (rather than the sort of person he or she is), which can lead to a feeling of worthlessness in the poor, or a desperate desire to get money at all costs.[20] Our ultimate goal, he says, should be "relationships governed by trust rather than financially mediated contracts; public space for the public rather than for consumers; media which are motivated to experiment, shun sensationalism and engage in serious debate, rather than simply chase ratings; and product manufacturers and consumers for whom ethical concerns are at least as important as price considerations."[21]

---

14. Ibid., 72.

15. Spencer, *The Measure of All Things?* 20–22.

16. Ibid., 22–24.

17. Ibid., 24–25.

18. Ibid., 25–26.

19. Ibid., 26.

20. Ibid., 26–27.

21. Ibid., 31.

Seeking a Better Means of Valuation

In a series of publications Philip Goodchild has developed the thesis that an alternative source of valuation is required if money is to be redeemed, the most extended treatment of which is to be found in his *Theology of Money* (2007). The key to Goodchild's whole argument lies in his recognition that money becomes "the value of all values." "Money posits itself as the universal, the supreme value, and the means of access to all other values. At the same time, money becomes a kind of encompassing membrane that determines what will be counted as valuable."[22] Even land is only valuable to the extent that it is valued in terms of money and can be changed into money.[23] The whole direction of movement in the economy is, in fact, to give monetary value to all possible items, including items previously thought to be common property (like water), and also so-called intellectual property. In this way, nonmarket economies are treated as belonging to a different order of reality. Such economies are only recognized insofar as they accept the use of money according to the rules of the capitalist system.

Goodchild's contention is that, instead of allowing exchange value to be the only measure of value, "political economy should be primarily concerned with the distribution of nutrition and time."[24] In this connection, he obviously has sympathy with the labor theory of value of Smith and Marx, but maintains "this is no longer credible when most energy for work is provided by fossil and nuclear fuels rather than human labour."[25] The problem, from the point of view of ethics, is that a money economy, if it is not regulated, is strictly amoral. It takes no account of human needs or human well-being, let alone the well-being of the cosmos. As propounded by Adam Smith, the capitalist economy operates on the basis of self-interest. In practice, people can operate from time to time with different motivations, but, once money has been allowed to take the role that it has been allowed to take in recent years, self-interest and the making of profit become the dominant factors. There would be the possibility of escape if legislation could be produced to limit the power of money. However, "the option of sovereign legislation presupposes that

22. Goodchild, *Theology of Money*, 60.

23. Ibid., 41–42.

24. Ibid., 138.

25. Ibid., 139

sovereign action remains possible in spite of the threat of capital flight. It also assumes the formation of public consciousness on the basis of truth and justice, given the capitalist domination of the media and educational institutions."[26]

Ultimately, what is required is that the true source of evaluations be found, not in money, but in God. "The alternative to this idolatry (of money) is to declare that God is the True, the Good and the Life. In this case, one takes one's orientation within the fields of knowledge, ethics and temporal experience from God."[27] And he summarizes the contrast like this:

> God and money are competing sources of credit. Each seeks to determine the value of values. Yet where God is presumed to have created the world as it is, money presumes to transform the world by dismantling and exhausting it, if necessary, in order to generate profits and repay debts. Where God presides over a world understood in terms of being or eternal forms, money presides over a world understood in terms of becoming or perpetual creative destruction. Where God embodies the moral virtue of generosity or grace, money embodies the moral virtue of honouring one's contracts and paying one's dues.[28]

Putting it another way,

> Money is inherently theological because it is a source of the value of values. . . . Where God may only serve as a basis for common consent and action for all those who truly believe, money may serve as a basis for common consent and action for those who share no belief apart from the efficacy of money. As the means of access to all other goals produced by collective action, money posits itself as the supreme value. It therefore evacuates all other values of significance and effectivity.[29]

And so Goodchild comes back continually to the need to find some other way of evaluating values than the money evaluations given in the present money economy. "For economic behaviour to change fundamentally, it is necessary to develop new mechanisms for distributing attention and imagination. . . . Excessive attention to prices and excessive

26. Ibid., 134.
27. Ibid., 208.
28. Ibid., 214–15.
29. Ibid., 222–23.

imagination of economic opportunities and threats may lead to a mode of behaviour that is unable to be receptive to that which matters."[30] In particular, this means looking for a different kind of credit. As the money economy has been created by human beings, he considers, however difficult it may be,

> there is nothing to prevent the invention of new forms of credit, contract and exchange. . . . (1) Credit must be given to that which is worthy of credit. . . . (2) The conflicting needs of sustainability and profit must be recognized. . . . (3) The divorce between the secular and the religious, between attending to treasure on earth and attending to treasure in heaven must be overcome. . . . Both material conditions of production and spiritual conditions of credit must replace the sovereignty of the self-reflective subject as the focus of attention.[31]

Goodchild leaves to nontheologians the task of discovering what institutions might need to be created for the making and implementing of new evaluations. For all their usefulness, he reckons that the various proposals made by many up till now for the creation of alternative currencies (such as Local Exchange Trading Schemes) have not actually addressed the root problem of the power of the money with which they have to compete.[32] Obviously, this is a colossal problem. On the other hand, until the problem is tackled, the world will continue to be subject to the imbalances and tyranny of the present system. Very tentatively, he suggests the need for a secondary tier of the economy concerned solely with the production and distribution of effective valuations. His hope would be that a time will come "when evaluative credits bear sufficient credit to count on their own merits, without being backed by a determinate reserve of hard monetary income."[33]

Practical Strategies

In terms of practical strategies for reforming money, the suggestions of Major Clifford Douglas in the early twentieth century remain significant. He advocated that all new money should be created by the state as credit

30. Ibid., 189.
31. Ibid., 242–43.
32. Ibid., 217n.
33. Ibid., 253.

to the whole community in the form of a "national dividend" payable to every citizen, on the basis of the claim that all could make to share in the common cultural heritage on which production is based. Producers would then sell their products at cost price (free of profit) and be compensated by credits allocated to them by the community.[34] It is not difficult to see that this puts the control of the economy in the hands of consumers (all consumers) rather than in the hands of a few producers or a few financiers; it could lead to a much more equitable distribution of resources, and the use of resources to meet general needs rather than luxuries for the more affluent (or even useless items that advertisers can persuade all classes of people to buy)—as well as providing a means for conserving the resources of the planet (rather than the exploitation that can result from the dominance of the profit motive). These proposals were very popular in the 1930s—and were even put into practice for a while in Alberta—but always encountered opposition from banks and from economists. From our present point of view, a major fruit of Douglas's proposals would have been to make money valuations much nearer to social value.

Fortunately, there are still those who are bending their minds to the problem. Richard Douthwaite (as we have already seen) has advocated the creation of an international currency (free of interest) based on units of energy to try and restrict growth to what is socially beneficial. Some of the latest proposals are those of Thomas Greco. Arguing that it is vital (for all the reasons already given) that a currency should not itself be a measure of value, but should serve only to facilitate the exchange of goods and services, Greco posits the creation of an independent (but objective) unit of account in terms of a basket of commodities, which should be (1) traded in one or more relatively free markets, (2) important in world trade, (3) important in satisfying basic human needs, (4) relatively stable in price (in real terms) over time, and (5) uniform in quality.[35]

Probably Goodchild is right that the baton has to be taken up by politicians and economists who are aware of the change of direction that is required—spurred on, one would hope, by voters with a similar awareness. My chief doubts, however, concern the plausibility of all proposals for the creation of a new kind of credit, either in place of money, or alongside it (except in very limited areas). In my own opinion, a far more

34. Douglas, *Social Credit*. A detailed assessment of Douglas's ideas can be found in Hutchinson and Burkitt, *The Political Economy of Social Credit and Guild Socialism*.

35. Greco, *The End of Money and the Future of Civilization*, 275–77.

plausible solution (in the first instance) could be found in a reassertion of the authority of national governments (and the invention of some kind of supra-national authority) to legislate for the control of money. There have been signs of progress on this in the aftermath of the crisis that began in 2007—in discussions by the G20 nations and in Barack Obama's attempts to control the U.S. banks—but it may take a lot more conviction (which may not come about, unfortunately, until there is a total collapse of the system) before we approach the drastic change that is actually required.

Such efforts might involve the proposals of writers like Nick Spencer, for instance, in terms of mandatory relational audits for all organizations over a certain size, regional banks, new currencies, serious reconsideration of the practice of lending at interest, challenging limited liability, and tax incentives focused on helping secure, robust, long-term relationships.[36] The New Economics Foundation, which has been in the forefront of attempts to chart the form of an alternative economy, advocates a process of "transition," the aim of which would be to build individual, social, and environmental value. This is in contrast with the value that is measured in Gross Domestic Product, which they claim "is ultimately perverse," as it only measures things that can be counted (including prisons, pollution, and weapons), rather than things that matter (such as caring and friendships). The first stage of this transition would be "the Great Revaluing," in which new measures of well-being (similar to the Human Development Index of the United Nations, or the Index of Sustainable Economic Welfare produced by Daly and Cobb) would be accepted, and then used to assess projects and programs. "In the Great Transition, this socially defined concept of value is placed at the centre of decision-making and progress towards it is measured. In public policy, achievement of such value would be instituted as the central goal."[37] In the private sector, businesses would be required to take full account of the costs of any (including unintended) consequences. "Through intelligent use of the tax system, the price paid by the final consumer would be aligned with real value."[38] We are already seeing the beginnings of this in the idea of carbon pricing.

36. Spencer, *The Measure of All Things?* 39–41.
37. New Economics Foundation, *The Great Transition*, 39.
38. Ibid.

The Theological Agenda

What then are the values that need to be promoted in place of valuation in terms of money? Tracing through the Old and New Testaments, the Scriptures assert, right at the beginning, the integrity (goodness) of creation, and in Genesis 2:15 that human beings were put in the Garden of Eden "to work it and take care of it" (NIV)—not just to "fill the earth and subdue it" (Genesis 1:28). In the Torah, I have already shown that the whole object seems to be to create a society where economic resources are shared, so that those who might otherwise be destitute are enabled to have the necessities of life (and a lot more). The establishment of a central government is initially resisted (1 Samuel 8), but is then accepted on the understanding that it is subject to the ultimate government of God and that it rules in the interests of the people (1 Samuel 10:25). In the New Testament, all this is universalized, so that each person is to love his or her neighbor as oneself—or, as Duchrow puts it, to act in "mutual service."[39]

The problem, throughout Christian history, has been to turn such basic values into prescriptions for practical action. One recent attempt can be seen in the "middle axiom" philosophy pursued by a number of British writers during the twentieth century—in particular by Ronald Preston. The phrase "middle axiom" was coined by J. H. Oldham, the veteran ecumenical statesman, in the preparatory volume for the Oxford Conference of 1937: "Between purely general statements of the ethical demands of the gospel and the decisions that have to be made in concrete situations there is need for what may be described as middle axioms."[40] Brought up in the tradition of Temple and Tawney, Preston's socialism was tempered by his pragmatic approach and his desire to give scope to the expertise of professional economists. His ideal situation was that a group of experts from different disciplines should work on a project together (as came increasingly to be the case in the Church of England and in the World Council of Churches). Preston sets out his case as follows:

> Once it is clear that we cannot proceed directly from the Christian tradition, whether the Bible or Natural Law or Systematic Theology, to conclusions in the spheres of various specialist studies, in this case economics, industry and politics, there is no escape from coming to grips with the empirical data in those fields and

39. Duchrow, *Alternatives to Global Capitalism*, 186.
40. Hooft and Oldham, *The Church and Its Function in Society*, 209–10.

mastering the various intellectual disciplines needed to cope with them; the moral theologian cannot do so on the basis of his discipline alone. Ideally, this is a co-operative enterprise, an interdisciplinary one.[41]

The chief middle axioms are, for Preston, very general concepts like *agape*, freedom, social fellowship, service, equality, justice, concern for the poor (or even "the responsible society" or "the just, participatory and sustainable society").[42] There is then, however, a further stage, where an attempt is made to get closer to particular situations, and this involves getting at "the facts" to find out "what is going on."[43] But Preston is realistic enough to recognize that this attempt will not always be successful—facts are "slippery things," different accounts may be given of the relevant facts, experts can sometimes be mistaken, different conclusions may be drawn by different people. "There is no suggestion that it will always be possible [to find middle axioms]; merely that it is important to try."[44]

Preston acknowledged criticisms of this approach, particularly by Duncan Forrester, which emanate from Liberation Theology and from more conservative theology—that the approach is elitist, that it springs "from an ivory tower misunderstanding of theology,"[45] and that the church should be able more often to ally itself with a detailed policy option. An interesting attempt to cut this Gordian knot is to be found in the movement to find a "global ethic" highlighted in the declaration *Toward a Global Ethic* by the Parliament of the World's Religions (1993). Several sections of this declaration go back to the Ten Commandments as "directives" in "the great religious and ethical traditions of mankind."[46] One section of the declaration covers "commitment to a culture of solidarity and a just economic order" and is based on the Seventh Commandment, "You shall not steal."[47] On this basis it is claimed that "in the developed countries, a distinction must be made between necessary and limitless consumption, between socially beneficial and unjustified uses of natural

41. Preston, *Religion and the Persistence of Capitalism*, 22.

42. Preston, *Church and Society in the Late Twentieth Century*, 148.

43. Ibid., 149

44. Ibid., 150

45. Ibid., 153.

46. Küng, *Yes to a Global Ethic*, 18.

47. Ibid., 20.

resources, and between a profit-only and a socially beneficial and ecologically oriented market economy."[48] These are noble aspirations. What is not stated, unfortunately, is how the Seventh Commandment can be said to have all these implications. There is an implied suggestion that a free-market economy is inconsistent with the commandment, but this is not specifically related to any theology of money.

Recent writers have been more positive than Preston, saying that specifically Christian principles should be proclaimed rather than added to the melting pot of secular ideas. So Stanley Hauerwas, for instance, praises the strong words of Pope John Paul II's encyclical, *Centesimus Annus* (1991).[49] Hauerwas has to admit, however, the inadequacy of the way that papal encyclicals have always been written "at a generalized level that makes their pronouncements seem platitudinous and/or irrelevant for policy decision."[50] The most effective work in this area in the last ten years has probably been that of the New Economics Foundation—but, for the most part, without stating specific Christian principles. So Ann Pettifor wrote *The Coming First World Debt Crisis* "to make the case that Western societies have to revive moral standards and set clear *ethical* benchmarks by which to regulate credit and debt, and to rein in the finance sector."[51] She did assert that "it is particularly important that Christian leaders should once again take up the cudgels against usury,"[52] but then proceeded without further religious reference.

In the last few years we have gotten used to the idea of "values"—that every group or tradition has a number of core beliefs that determine accepted behavior. Gradually it has been appreciated that the truth about "Christian values" is that they may often be in conflict with the values of the total community within which Christians live. If this is true anywhere, it must be true of the economic realm, dominated as it is in these days by the values of the free market. In advocating scriptural values, Christians will not necessarily expect to convince all their hearers, but that doesn't mean that they should keep quiet. Moreover, if their contribution is made in a sensitive way, they may find themselves sounding notes that resonate

48. Ibid., 21.

49. Hauerwas, "In Praise of *Centesimus Annus*," 416–32.

50. Ibid., 416.

51. Pettifor, *The Coming First World Debt Crisis*, 13.

52. Ibid., 14.

with people of quite different philosophies.[53] Any future economic system influenced by Christian values is bound to look very different from the economy of today. It is the assertion of this chapter that Christian values have much to contribute to the re-formation of money that is so much needed. In particular, it is vital that we move beyond the situation where monetary value is a dominant element.

---

53. As in Biggar, "God in Public Reason," 9–19.

CHAPTER SIX

Money and Desire

DESIRE, IN THE SENSE of longing after what you do not at present possess, is obviously one of the great motivators of human action, almost on a par with the instinct for self-preservation. It could be said that it has led to much of human progress. In the New Testament, the Greek word *epithumia* expresses any intense longing, which is only condemned if it is misdirected or excessive.[1] In the majority of its occurrences, however, it carries a negative connotation—i.e., with the meaning of evil desire or lust. The danger of this kind of desire has been appreciated (probably) in all cultures and in every stage of human history. E. F. Schumacher, for instance, in a discussion of Buddhist economics, says that "the Buddhist sees the essence of civilization not in a multiplication of wants, but in the purification of the human character."[2] From this viewpoint, selfish desire is the most dangerous motivation in the human heart, and it is possible to view the whole purpose of the Buddhist religion as an attempt to control it. This chapter will look at the relationship between desire and money, particularly as it is described in Christian theology.

Desire and Christian Thinking

In the third chapter of the book of Genesis, devoted to what is sometimes called "the Fall," the text seeks to demonstrate how (apart from Satan) it was desire that was the cause of the original separation of human beings from God.[3] If one takes the passage as myth (which I do), the message

1. Grayston, "Desire," 64.
2. Schumacher, *Small Is Beautiful*, 46.
3. "When the woman saw that the fruit of the tree was good for food and pleasing to

could be that this continues to be true, and thus the cause of many of the troubles experienced by both women[4] and men[5]. This message gives great significance to the fact that the last of the Ten Commandments of Judaism is devoted to coveting, or desiring that which belongs rightfully to another (Exodus 20:17). While the previous nine commandments are exhortations to different kinds of conduct (or to abstaining from different kinds of conduct), the tenth goes behind conduct to the psychological impulses of desire. Throughout the Old Testament literature (and especially in the prophets) there are many exhortations to avoid coveting that which belongs to someone else. The stoning of Achan after the battle of Jericho is attributed to his coveting what belonged to God (Joshua 7:21)—the severity of the punishment indicating a fear of what might happen if looting got out of control. Desire for dishonest gain is condemned in Proverbs 28:16 and Jeremiah 6:13.

In the New Testament, desire is clearly designated as one of the chief motivators of human activity. Jesus is not interested so much in actions as in their motivations. In his Beatitudes—which take the place in his Sermon on the Mount occupied by the Ten Commandments in "The Book of the Covenant" (Exodus 20–23)—the blessed are those who exhibit certain attributes, rather than those who live according to certain laws. So, for instance, "Blessed are those who hunger and thirst after righteousness" (Matthew 5:6)—those with a certain motivation rather than those who observe certain laws. Throughout his ministry Jesus is combating the legalism exhibited especially by the Pharisees, whom he condemns, not so much for what they were doing, as for the motivations of their hearts. The commandments themselves are summarized in terms of love toward God and neighbor (Matthew 22:37–40). In Mark 7:1–23, Jesus points to the attitudes resident in the heart as what make a person unclean—among which he includes greed and envy. In Matthew 6:19–21, he talks of storing up treasures in heaven in preference to treasures on earth: "for where your treasure is, there your heart will be also."

This emphasis is then taken up by the writers of the New Testament letters, where the control of evil desires is seen as one of the chief ways to right living. "Put to death, therefore, whatever belongs to your earthly

the eye, and also desirable for gaining wisdom, she took some and ate it. She also gave some to her husband, and he ate it" (Genesis 3:6).

4. Genesis 3:16.

5. Genesis 3:17–19.

nature . . . evil desires and greed, which is idolatry" (Colossians 3:5). "People who want to get rich fall into temptation and a trap and into many foolish and harmful desires that plunge men into ruin and destruction" (1 Timothy 6:9).

In the meantime, there had developed a parallel discussion of desire in the works of the Greek philosophers, and especially Aristotle. Aristotle defines desire as "a form of appetite."[6] Such an appetite is not necessarily to be regarded negatively. In fact, to desire what is good is the means by which humanity makes progress. It is to be regarded negatively when it is indulged to excess. Because the desires of the human heart are infinite, therefore, they have to be curbed. This thinking was taken into Christianity by Augustine, and later by the scholastics. So, in the teaching of Aquinas, "the affective part of our souls is moved towards an attractive object; and the satisfying of desire is joy."[7] Gorringe observes that "the point of both the Greek and the Christian traditions is that desire may be energy, but it is not undifferentiated. It requires distinctions."[8] He then suggests, following the work of Deleuze and Guattari, that "the distinction between real desire and desire posing as egoism is central to the critique of capitalism, which rests on a distinction between needlessly stimulated desires on the one hand and real needs on the other."[9]

In fact, the New Testament has a separate word *philarguria* to refer to love of money (1 Timothy 6:10), along with *philargurioi* (2 Timothy 3:2; Luke 16:14) for lovers of money. First Timothy 6:10 is a verse that has been quoted (and mis-quoted) on numerous occasions: "For the love of money is the root of all evil" (1 Timothy 6:10 AV, RSV). In this translation, this extraordinary unqualified statement bypasses numerous other candidates for the role of the root cause of evil (such as the love of pleasure or the satisfaction of selfish desires in general). Franz Hinkelammert has no hesitation in accepting this translation at face value: "The root of all evil lies in love of money—the money god . . . drags its victims down to ruin and destruction."[10] As we have seen, a translation now more in vogue, however, is that "the love of money is a root of all kinds of evil"

6. Aristotle, *On the Soul*, para. 10.

7. Aquinas, *Summa Theologica*, part I, 2nd part, 26.2, as summarized in Gorringe, *Education of Desire*, 89.

8. Gorringe, *Education of Desire*, 90.

9. Ibid.

10. Hinkelammert, *Ideological Weapons of Death*, 140.

(as niv and other modern versions). Donald Guthrie echoes other writers in pointing out that there is no definite article before "root." Even without the definite article, however, "root" occupies the place of emphasis in the sentence, which could justify the traditional translation. Guthrie falls back eventually on the assertion that "it must not be deduced from this that the love of money is the sole root of all evil, for the New Testament does not support this."[11] So also J. N. D. Kelly: "It is extravagant to assert that love of money is the root cause of all sins"[12]—and George W. Knight III: "This is borne out by Paul's previous use of *pantes* for all sorts of human beings rather than for each and every person."[13] What this verse does, however, is to encapsulate a suspicion of the temptations aroused by money, which took deep root in the Christian church and which has survived for most of the Christian era.

A Dialectical Relationship

When we come to consider the precise relationship between money and desire, we should probably consider it as a dialectical (two-way) relationship. On the one hand, money is a measure of desire. On the other, it is a creator of desire.

Aristotle expressed the first aspect of the relationship when he talked of money as the measure of need (or demand):

> All goods to be exchanged should be measurable by some standard coin or measure. In reality, this measure is the need which holds all things together; for if man had no needs at all or no needs of a similar nature, there would be no exchange or not this kind of exchange. So a coin is a sort of substitute [or representative] for need.[14]

In technical economic terms this should be extended to refer to demand *in relation to supply*, in that price is not determined simply by demand. A longstanding tradition (from the scholastics to Marx) has sought to argue that the price of an object is (and should be) determined by the costs involved in its production (and especially the costs of labor). In the absence of regulations to enforce this, however, and with the dominating

11. Guthrie, *The Pastoral Epistles*, 113–14.
12. Kelly, *A Commentary on the Pastoral Epistles*, 138.
13. Knight, *The Pastoral Epistles*, 258.
14. Aristotle, *Nicomachean Ethics*, bk. E, sec. 8, p. 86.

influence of monopolies, the reality has always been very different. In a totally free market, demand is *the* controlling factor. Without demand, production is senseless. In these circumstances, price measured in terms of money *is* largely a reflection of demand.

The second aspect of their relationship—money as the creator of desire—has a long history. Jacques Ellul points out that the Hebrew word for money, *kesef*, comes from a verb meaning "to desire, to languish after something." He comments, "This implies that, right from the beginning, when the Hebrew language was being formed, the spiritual character of money as well as its power was already stressed."[15] Emphasizing money's encouragement of evil desire, one of the characters in Sophocles's Antigone says:

> Nothing so evil as money ever grew to be current among men.
> This lays cities low, this drives men from their homes, this trains
> and warps honest souls till they set themselves to works of shame;
> this still teaches folk to practice villainies, and to know every god-
> less deed.[16]

James Buchan says, "Here, at the dawn of money men already recognize its deepest meaning: that money, because it has the potential to fulfil any mortal purpose and convey any mortal desire, becomes the absolute purpose and the object of the most intense desire it can convey."[17] He quotes Schopenhauer as regarding it as inevitable: "Men are often criticized in that money is the chief object of their wishes and is preferred above all else, but it is natural, even unavoidable. For money is an inexhaustible Proteus, ever ready to change itself into the present object of our changeable wishes and manifold needs."[18] Rudolf Bahro expresses this in forthright terms when he says, "Right from the beginning money has had an *autonomous* logic, which was never directed toward those purposes which, in the spirit of an 'original moral economy', it should have obeyed."[19] Bahro considers that the chief desires of the human being are centered in one's need for recognition and adornment, and that for this purpose (as we saw in the last chapter) "money is the ideal means, for it can be traded for absolutely anything: power, property, prestige, personality."[20]

15. Ellul, *Money and Power*, 51.

16. *The Antigone*, lines 295-300; part 3 in Jebb, *Sophocles: The Plays and Fragments*.

17. Buchan, *Frozen Desire*, 31.

18. Ibid.

19. Bahro, *Avoiding Social and Ecological Disaster*, 106.

20. Ibid.

An Alternative Vision

The only way out, according to Bahro, is a spiritual revolution. He doesn't have great hopes for it, recognizing the hold that money has on everyone. But he takes us back to the teaching of Jesus when he says, "If we were all able to feel what Jesus experienced when he said that we should give as little thought to food and clothing as do the birds of the air and the lilies of the field, then abolition of the money economy would be near, and a form of human existence approaching a balance with the rest of nature would be secured."[21] In the teaching of Jesus, this passage is another part, of course, of his Sermon on the Mount, where he is describing what life will be like in the kingdom he has come to reveal. In the kingdom that Jesus is establishing, money will be subservient to God and to his purposes. So insignificant will it be, in fact, that those who share its values will not need to fear about the necessities of life. These will not be dependent on how much money one has. They will be provided by the merciful and generous Father whose kingdom it is. To be anxious about such things is the characteristic attitude of those who don't know God. But those who know God as their perfect heavenly Father have no need to fear. "Seek first his kingdom and his righteousness, and all these things will be given to you as well" (Matthew 6:33).

Martin Hengel considers that Jesus's "free attitude to property" is based on his conviction of the imminence of the coming of the kingdom (rather like Paul in 1 Corinthians 7:26–31).[22] This is based, however, on the idea that somehow the kingdom is present, though only "in a hidden way," in the work of Jesus. The fact is that, though the consummation of the kingdom may yet be ahead of us, the kingdom was inaugurated and demonstrated in numerous ways in the ministry of Jesus. Jesus's attitude to possessions, therefore, was determined rather by the presence of the kingdom than by its imminence. What he is saying is that it is our fear about not having enough and our lack of trust in God that pushes us into the service of mammon.[23] It could even be argued (as Bahro would certainly do) that it is anxiously seeking more and more that is the source of the severe ecological (and financial) problems of the present day. If,

---

21. Ibid., 110.

22. Hengel, *Property and Riches in the Early Church*, 26–30.

23. Gay, *Cash Values*, 89.

instead, we were seeking to fulfill God's will, doing what is just, and trusting in his grace, we would be much less likely to suffer these problems.

What cannot be avoided is that some of Jesus's hardest words were reserved for those who had riches. Take, for instance, the hardest (in Matthew 19:16–26 and parallels), where Jesus tells the rich young man that he must sell all his possessions and give to the poor, and then says to his disciples that it is easier for a camel to go through the eye of a needle than for a rich man to enter the kingdom of God. There continues to be much debate as to whether these commands are universally applicable.[24] For myself, following D. E. Nineham,[25] I take it that, though these appear to be categorical statements, they need to be taken in the context of the whole of Jesus's teaching, where receiving eternal life and entering the kingdom heaven are open to all, regardless of their status. Rather, in this particular situation, Jesus is forcing the rich young man to face up to the fact of his love of riches, which have become his god (thus breaking the first commandment) or an idol (breaking the second), and urging him to demonstrate the total commitment to God that faith requires. Then, in his typical hyperbole, he is telling his disciples how very difficult it is for a rich man to enter the kingdom. When his disciples complain, "Who then can be saved?" Jesus replies. "With man this is impossible, but with God all things are possible," implying that, though it is difficult, it is not totally impossible.

We need in a similar way to understand Jesus' condemnation of the rich in Luke 6:24, "Woe to you who are rich, for you have already received your comfort"—not that riches are wrong in themselves, but that they can so easily lead their possessors to trust in their riches rather than in God. So also his words to his disciples in Luke 14:33, "Any of you who does not give up everything that he has cannot be my disciple"—not that a disciple has literally to give up everything he has, but that it has to take second place in his affections to his love for God. In the same vein, I would interpret the disciples' leaving "everything" to follow Jesus (Luke 5:11 and 28) as an indication of their commitment to Jesus rather than an absolute requirement for all disciples.

Though he may not have regarded money/riches as intrinsically evil, there are, nevertheless, numerous passages where Jesus refers to the

24. Matera, *New Testament Ethics*, 80–82.

25. Nineham, *Gospel of Mark*, 231–32.

dangers they present. So, for instance, in Mark 4:19 Jesus refers to "the deceitfulness of wealth" as one of those things which hinder the growth of the Word of God in a person's soul. In the Sermon on the Mount he says, "Do not store up for yourself treasures on earth, where moth and rust destroy, and where thieves break in and steal. But store up for yourselves treasures in heaven, where moth and rust do not destroy, and where thieves do not break in and steal. For where your treasure is, there your heart will be also" (Matthew 6:19–21). As we have already seen, (like Britain's queen) he carried no money with him (though Judas looked after a communal purse)—so that money required for the temple tax had to be found in the mouth of a fish (Matthew 17:27). When he sent his disciples out to preach, he told them not to "take along any gold or silver or copper" in their belts (Matthew 10:9). And then we have to take seriously his assertion that it is impossible to serve both God and Mammon.

An Untidy History

In the history of the Christian church it has to be recognized that Jesus's attitude to money has often been ignored. When Christianity became the official religion of the Roman Empire, a revolution took place, in that, for the first time, the church was allowed to hold property. At first, they acquired only places of worship and burial grounds. By the fourth century, however, through the generous donations of emperors and other benefactors, the church possessed large estates all over the empire. In AD 470, an imperial decree banned the alienation of church properties, thus ensuring the landed wealth of the church for the foreseeable future. Then, once the clergy had become a salaried profession, they also became landowners, and lay Christians often became possessors of large estates. A reaction set in with the ascetic movement and the founding of monasteries. Almost inevitably, however, with the great resources they acquired through the many bequests made to them and the special favors granted them by local rulers, the monasteries became very rich and began to get involved in trade. Initially, they worked through middlemen, then through lay brothers. Eventually, however, they became involved on a large scale. Lester Little comments, "Monasticism was thus offered the eternal choice between God and Mammon, and the temptation in many cases was irresistible."[26]

26. Little, *Religious Poverty and the Profit Economy in Medieval Europe*, 323.

I have already referred to the irony that the scholastics and Calvin, who were desperately seeking to maintain a path of moderation, should have ultimately provided the rationale that would encourage the frantic seeking after money that was to characterize the great trade expansion of their time. Moderation was eventually trodden under foot. Probably the greatest cause of its demise was the far greater availability of luxury goods made possible through the adventures of the traders (now usually described as "discoverers") who extended so greatly European awareness of the rest of the world. As is observed by McKendrick and colleagues in *The Birth of a Consumer Society*, it was not the desire to consume that was new, it was the ability to do so.[27] In the first instance, such items were imported rather than locally produced. The ensuing Industrial Revolution, however, was built on the same foundation. From one point of view, one should concentrate, perhaps, on the desire for wealth that inspired the merchants and the industrialists. Equally significant, however, was the desire to consume their goods. And, justifying both were the theorists like Locke and Adam Smith, who encouraged both trade and consumption as the means to achieving "the wealth of nations."

Of great influence at the time was Bernard Mandeville (1670?–1733) with his *Fable of the Bees* (1714) in which he likened an economy to a hive of bees. In this hive, all the bees were driven by lust and vanity, but even the poorest was better off than they would have been on their own. The reason was that consumption produces employment (e.g., even burglars produce work for locksmiths). Then one day a Puritan revolution took place. Crime and military spending ceased, and luxury was spurned. The result was unemployment and the collapse of entire industries. Many bees left the hive.[28] In a similar way, Adam Smith argued that, even though our commercial actions may be taken from selfish motives, this will work out for the general benefit. "It is not from the benevolence of the butcher, the brewer, or the baker that we expect our dinner, but from their regard to their own interest. We address ourselves, not to their humanity, but to their self-love."[29] Behind it all is "an invisible hand" by which the general interest is promoted.[30] It can be argued that Smith recognizes the importance of such values as truth, honesty, obligation, and trust in the proper

27. McKendrick, Brewer, and Plumb, *Birth of a Consumer Society*, 2.
28. Mandeville, "The Fable of the Bees" (1714).
29. Smith, *Wealth of Nations*, bk. 1, ch. 2, p. 119.
30. Ibid., bk. 4, ch. 2, p. 32.

working of an economy (as in his book *The Moral Sentiments*). Unfortunately, however, the economy he is describing tends to lead to the erosion of just these values and to an encouragement of naked self-interest.

Contemporary Analysis

The first great analysis of the consumer society was by Thomas Veblen in *The Theory of the Leisure Class* (1899), in which he viewed capitalism as based on chronic dissatisfaction associated with "emulative consumption." Whereas the conventional wisdom held that the purpose of acquiring goods was to consume them, he maintained that, right from the beginning, "the motive that lies at the root of ownership is emulation."[31] For the first in the queue, the motive might be that of acquiring status. But, after that, it is the emulation of those already having status. This is not to overlook the fact that, especially for the poorer members of society, much acquisition may be for the purposes of survival. However, as far as status is concerned, it is the ownership of property that counts. And, once workers have sufficient for survival, this is the motive that increasingly moves them. All of which, of course, is to their ultimate disadvantage, in that it works to preserve the existing economic system and to keep working people in subjection to it.

In *The Acquisitive Society* (1921), R. H. Tawney began from an observation that, whatever may have been the case in the past, "modern societies aim at protecting economic rights."[32] "Such societies may be called Acquisitive Societies, because their whole tendency and interest and preoccupation is to promote the acquisition of wealth."[33] One result of this preoccupation is the overproduction of luxury goods for those with the most money, while the working man "is employed in making goods which no-one can make with happiness, or indeed without loss of self-respect, because he knows that they had much better not be made, and that his life is wasted in making them."[34] What Tawney wanted to see

---

31. Veblen, *Theory of the Leisure Class*, 25.
32. Tawney, *Acquisitive Society*, 31.
33. Ibid., 32.
34. Ibid., 38.

was a society organized primarily for the performance of duties, rather than the maintenance of rights.[35]

By the time J. K. Galbraith wrote *The Affluent Society* in 1958, the United States had reached a degree of affluence that, even if inequality remained, the great concern had become the production of goods, such that the Gross Domestic Product was the essential measure of economic vitality. But, in order to keep consumer demand at the level necessary for production to continue to grow, the situation had emerged where demand had to be encouraged by producers, particularly by means of advertising. "Production, not only passively through emulation, but actively through advertising and related activities, creates the wants it seeks to satisfy."[36] But this begs the question of whether increasing production of this sort is really the route to the happiness of all.

The brute fact is that the capitalist system, especially where the markets (and money) are free, appears to lock us into an endless seeking after that which (eventually) does not satisfy. As I have indicated earlier, a system based on debt and interest *needs* to be growing continually simply to repay debts and pay interest (let alone to produce profits and money for re-investment). Individual firms, if they are to survive, are on the same treadmill. By one means or another, therefore, the consumer has to be persuaded to keep on buying. There are numerous strategies for achieving this: inbuilt obsolescence, more advanced products, credit cards, loyalty cards, special offers, to name but a few.

Above all, of course, there is advertising, some of which we don't even recognize as such—including so-called subliminal advertising, which appeals at a very deep level. Ralph Glasser, author of *The New High Priesthood*, puts it pithily when he says, "Marketing does not sell a product—it sells a dream, a dream of beauty, of health, of success, of power."[37] It is particularly powerful in the lives of the poor (seeking consolation) and the young (seeking identity). Wilkinson and Pickett are able to show (sadly) that, where inequality is greatest, it "ratchets up the competitive pressure to consume"—indeed, "inequality increases spending on advertising."[38] Governments, sadly, do little to combat it—even in relation to what is

---

35. Ibid., 80.
36. Galbraith, *The Affluent Society*, 130.
37. Glasser, *The New High Priesthood*, 12.
38. Wilkinson and Pickett, *The Spirit Level*, 227–28.

known to be harmful (like smoking or alcohol). Their economies are dependent on continual growth (quite apart from the votes of consumers).

Jung Mo Sung, in his recent book *Desire, Market and Religion*, locates much of the problem in the confusion between needs and desire. What we are persuaded by advertisers is that we need an endless variety of products. But the truth is our actual needs are limited. What are unlimited are our desires.[39] Sung says, "When one thinks from the standpoint of desires, there are no limits. One pursues the limitless. And when one desires the limitless there is never anything left to share. There is never enough."[40] The tragedy of the contemporary experience is that all this is exploited by the big players in the capitalist economy for their own ends. It is even justified by neoliberal thinkers as the engine of progress[41]—to the extent that even the poor are persuaded to accept sacrifices when the system is in trouble so that "progress" can continue[42] (as we are seeing now in the aftermath of the recent crisis of the system). The ultimate tragedy is that an economy based on the satisfaction of desires will lead inevitably to the destruction of the planet.[43]

Conclusions

Christianity (along with Judaism) refutes this logic by its distinction between needs and desire and by its recognition that there *are* limits to what we may desire. As we have already seen, both the Old and New Testaments require us to put the well-being of others before the satisfaction of our own desires. Scripture also recognizes the role played by money in the stimulation of desire, and commands us to make money our servant rather than our master. Sung is concerned about how the immense power of mimetic desire can be curbed. He proposes, first of all, the *unmasking* of the mechanisms that control the modern economy. Then he suggests the encouraging of a different type of mimetic desire, namely, the desire to emulate the persons of integrity (like St. Francis) that we could take

---

39. Sung, *Desire, Market and Religion*, 32.

40. Ibid., 33.

41. Ibid., 37.

42. Ibid., 42–44.

43. Ibid., 67.

as models of a different way.[44] In the end, as Bahro realizes, desire needs to be converted; we need "a new spirituality that changes the desires by changing the desire's model."[45]

At the same time there is always the possibility of changing those aspects of the system that trade on desire. If there is one thing that seems to have struck home as a result of the recent economic crisis, it is that it was brought about by excessive desire. Much has been said about the greed of the bankers and the bonuses awarded them for making short-term profits that bore no relation to the underlying realities of the economy. It has also been realized, however, that their customers have been equally at fault in seeking such enormous levels of credit—not to mention the governments and regulators who turned a blind eye. Not surprisingly, perhaps, it has been in this area that Christian spokespersons have had most to say. But, as St. Paul, recognized, moralizing by itself gets you nowhere. Joerg Rieger suggests (following Marx), that the key, in the end, is actually not so much in the area of consumption as in production. For him, the goal of socialism is not that rich people should share with poor people. Charity is not enough. In fact, appealing to charity can disguise the need for systemic change. "Rather the goal of socialism is to consciously manage economic activity with an eye to maximizing collective economic well-being, rather than individual profit. . . . everything else follows from this, including the production and reproduction of desire and the fulfilment of human need."[46] Citing the saying of Jesus, "Strive first for the kingdom of God and his righteousness [justice] and all these things [food, drink, clothes] will be given to you as well" (Matthew 6:33), he concludes: "Relationships of production that are just, where all can contribute according to their abilities—the 'kingdom of God and his justice'—create a situation where human needs are met and where human sin is addressed in realistic fashion."[47] One does not need to move from this to the necessity of a totalitarian state, but such an understanding does require considering theological principles as central to all policy-making, rather than acceding to the impulses of human desire focused on money.

44. Ibid., 48–49.
45. Ibid., 75.
46. Rieger, *No Rising Tide*, 119.
47. Ibid., 119–20.

But money is extremely powerful, and I move from here to consider, through the insights of Christian theology, how it achieves such power and how such power can be contained.

CHAPTER SEVEN

Money and Power

THE FOURTH (AND FINAL) standpoint from which I am surveying the institution of money is in respect of power. I refer in this context to the experience of human beings as subject to the power exercised upon them by outside forces or persons. Though the preceding chapters have demonstrated many ways in which the use of money can have negative antisocial effects, my conviction is that this is demonstrated most clearly in the power relationships that money encourages and fosters, which can result in nothing less than the oppression of the weak by the powerful.

In recent years it is the French philosopher Michel Foucault who has investigated most comprehensively the way in which power is exercised in different life situations. For him every action and every historical event is seen as an exercise in the exchange of power—as evidence of power relations.[1] The report of the Doctrine Commission of the Church of England, *Being Human*, devotes a whole chapter to the subject. Recognizing that power has come increasingly to be understood in a negative way, the writers are honest enough to admit the degree to which the Christian church has contributed to this through its own hierarchical structures, as well as its involvement in the Crusades, the Inquisition, etc. At the same time, they are anxious to emphasize how power can be used positively, that God himself exercises his power for the benefit of human beings, and that Jesus exercised his power in humility and in service. "In the Christian view power cannot be seen as intrinsically corrupt. To be created by God entails being gifted with human powers, the wise use of which is integral to being fully human. To be redeemed by God entails living in the light of

---

1. See especially Foucault, "The Subject and Power."

the power of the Resurrection. To be sanctified by God entails enjoyment and exercise of the gifts of the Holy Spirit."[2]

The writers draw attention (as others have done) to an ambiguity in the notion of power, not least as the word is used in the English language, which is clarified by the distinction in classical Greek between *dynamis* and *exousia*, the first having reference to strength, and the second to authority. In considering the power of money, it is necessary to keep both aspects in mind—that money has the strength to achieve much, but that it can also become a focus of domination. Few would doubt that money has the strength to achieve great things, and many would claim that the justification for the role of money in the capitalist system is that it has been able to achieve so much. It will be the contention of this chapter, however (while not contesting this fact), that money, particularly where it is allowed free rein, can exercise an authority that is often unjustifiable in Christian or moral terms.

The Power of Money

There are now very few economies that are not monetized (where all commodities are valued in terms of money). Once money attains this eminence, it exerts enormous power over the lives of all citizens. In 1844, Karl Marx wrote, "By possessing the property of buying everything, by possessing the property of appropriating all objects, money is thus the object of eminent possession. The universality of its property is the omnipotence of its being. It is, therefore, regarded as omnipotent."[3] If he were living today, he would say it with even greater emphasis.

Stephen Green wrote in 1996, "What is new about the last two decades is the sheer scale of the markets and the speed at which they are evolving. The flow of international capital has grown from a trickle to a flood which no government on earth can now dam."[4] In other words, the vast financial markets are now quite beyond the control of national governments and exercise enormous power in their own right. Further estimates are given by Richard Burnet and John Cavanagh: "In 1973 the gross sum in Eurocurrency accounts all over the world was US$315 bil-

2. Doctrine Commission, *Being Human*, 53–54.
3. Marx, "The Power of Money in Bourgeois Society," 166.
4. Green, *Serving God? Serving Mammon?* 7.

lion; by 1987 the total was nearly US$4 trillion"[5]—and by Ian Linden: "The daily turnover of currency transactions in the markets in the 1970s was about $1000 million; it is now well above $1,000,000 million, more than a hundred times the currency reserves of the world's governments put together."[6] Most of these transactions are speculative in nature.

What this vast quantitative change has actually brought about is a great qualitative change—money is no longer a servant, but a master. This can be seen, for instance, in the way in which the value of a currency is invariably the major consideration of those administering national finances. The decision of the new Labour government in 1997 to hand over decisions concerning Bank Rate to the Bank of England can be seen as handing over to financiers the most important tool for controlling the whole economy—even though their assignment is meant to be limited strictly to the control of inflation. In the same way, in the sphere of business, it is the value of the company's shares that is the main consideration in its board's and executives' decisions. In fact, it is the widely held assumption that it is "the ultimate or primary purpose of a company to maximize the value it creates for its shareholders,"[7] and executives who seek to follow other courses of action can be held to have abused their trust. There are, obviously, other ways of running a company. Some are investigating various "stakeholder" alternatives. Some investors are considering various possibilities of "ethical" investment. What cannot be denied, however, is that, for the most part, it is considerations centered on money that govern myriads of decisions in national and business life.

Sources of Money's Power

In the light of the last two chapters, it would be possible to discern a fairly straightforward route to the power possessed by money, beginning from the way that money (at least in a developed economy) is the means by which everything is valued (chapter 5), through the way in which money is the chief motivator for desire (chapter 6). I want to argue, however, that there is another deeper explanation.

---

5. Burnet and Cavanagh, "Electronic Money and the Casino Economy," 66.

6. Linden, "Globalization and the Church," 4.

7. Nussbaum, "Does Shareholder Value Drive the World?" 37.

I have already argued that, even in a barter situation, those involved in barter are evaluating the commodities involved in relation to some notional "money of account." I have also argued that money should not be considered in isolation from other kinds of property (such as land). If we understand "mammon," therefore, as Jesus might have understood it in the first century AD, it would almost certainly have referred to land and other property, even more than to gold and silver, or other commodities used as means of exchange. On this basis, there is evidence right through the Old Testament period of the power of money, where I have drawn attention to the way in which those sometimes described as elites were able to use money to exercise power over those less fortunate than themselves—which the prophets described (often quite openly) as injustice and oppression. This tradition was continued by Jesus himself, and much of his ministry can be interpreted as an attempt to get those who were using money in this way to appreciate what they were doing and to repent. The classic example was his turning over the tables of the moneychangers and of those who sold goods in the temple precincts. Having considered the early church Fathers and their attitude to property, and the efforts of the scholastics to find a just price for everything, it can easily be appreciated that, behind all their discussions, was a concern about the power exercised by those in possession of money over those whose lack of money left them vulnerable.

As we have already seen, in the early modern period the unequal sharing of property even came to be *justified* by writers like Locke and Adam Smith. Where indignation rose again it was as a result of the conditions to which many were subjected in the Industrial Revolution, and it can be seen particularly in the writings of Karl Marx. To many who witnessed the dramatic growth of the nineteenth century, money was the oil that enabled the great Industrial Revolution to roll. Marx, however, saw the anguish of numerous working people trapped in situations from which they could only by superhuman efforts extricate themselves, locked into a money economy that failed to provide their basic human needs. When they had lived in the countryside, many of them had lived in their own houses, on their own land, growing on that land the food they needed to keep them fit and well. But as they lost their house or their land, they were forced to rely on money to rent a place in which to live and to buy the food they needed to eat. And this meant signing on to work for wages. Very often your employer had you at his mercy, paying you less than a living wage. And, if anything went wrong, if you were ill or lost your job for any reason, you could be destitute.

Marx developed at great length his theories about the functioning of an industrial society and the place of money in it. His conclusion was that, once you are involved in the money economy, your relations with other people rest on an entirely new basis, and you lose control, to a greater or lesser extent, of your own future. It is, in fact, the chief argument of this book that, as soon as anyone makes a transaction involving the use of money, he or she enters a world in which one is no longer free. In the process of barter, each participant in a transaction emerges with a commodity that can be used directly for the betterment of one's life. Where someone has sold a commodity in exchange for money, however, the seller emerges with a commodity (money) that cannot be used directly for the betterment of his or her life. The money now possessed (it is true) can be used for an infinite number of purposes, *but only in accordance with the rules that control its use.*

Contrary to widespread belief, money is not, in fact, neutral. It can even be said to make us its slaves. In the words of Jacques Ellul, "We can, if we must, use money, but it is really money that uses us and makes us its servants by bringing us under its law and subordinating us to its aims."[8] It is not enough to say that money can be used for good or evil. If it is left uncontrolled, as is advocated in the contemporary philosophy of neoliberalism, an economy based on money can have all kinds of evil effects. This is, in practice, why both national governments and international agencies (even if they profess to follow many neoliberal policies) have no option but to regulate many ways in which money is allowed to function. The most significant problem in our modern world that arises directly from the existence of money is the widespread incidence of interest-bearing credit, which, as debt, has a crippling effect on the lives of individuals and nations.

It can be argued, of course, that any involvement in trading involves danger, so that it is not money itself that is the problem, but the conditions of trading at any particular time. Even in a barter situation (where there is no money involved), it could be said, if you have a product on which you have spent a lot of labor, but which you cannot exchange, you may be in trouble. Or if "the terms of trade" turn against you, so that your

8. Ellul, *Money and Power*, 76.

product can only be exchanged for small quantities of other products, you may be in trouble. However, there are particular dangers if you are exchanging your product for money. For instance, the value of the currency you are using may fall. If your money is held in a currency that is weak in relation to other currencies, you may suddenly find that you can buy very little with it. If it is held in shares, these may lose their value. If it is held as a bank deposit, the credibility of your bank may falter, and the bank could even collapse.

To put it in other words, money never exists in isolation. Its use and its value depend on its conditions of use—which are determined by the authority that gives it its validity. In a country like Britain, for instance, these conditions are determined ultimately by the law of the land and any lesser authorities to which authority is deputed—especially commercial banks, building societies, and insurance companies. Immediately, this gives the lie to the idea that any market can be free. It is only free within the limits that have been established for it, and these limits are almost always established by the possessors of money, who have an interest in establishing those limits to their own advantage.

This argument was first made substantially by Karl Polanyi in *The Great Transformation*, when he argued that laissez faire was actually *planned*[9]—on the basis that, at all stages of history, the market has been constructed, not from the free play of individual actors, but from the efforts of governments and others powerful enough to organize it (usually for their own interests). So Arthur MacEwan, when considering the suggestion that things should be "left to the market," insists that markets are historically constructed, and that governments have intervened massively at all stages of history. "In any society, the state plays the central role in defining markets by virtue of its importance in determining property rights, establishing social and physical infrastructure, and affecting the distribution of income and wealth."[10] If the argument is, therefore, that markets in the twenty-first century should be unfettered, we are not talking about markets that have evolved in some kind of natural way, but markets that have been constructed by government regulation, often for the benefit of those who have had the power to control them. A capitalist free-market system, for instance, is not the only possible system. It is a particular sys-

9. Polanyi, *The Great Transformation*, 139–40.

10. MacEwan, *Neo-Liberalism or Democracy?* 109.

tem created by those who have had the power to do so. "When markets serve their allocation functions, when they perform their 'magic', they do not do so in some independent or 'natural' way. Allocation of goods and resources through markets is not an alternative to conscious human intervention in economic affairs. Markets are the mechanism through which that intervention is organized."[11]

In practice, MacEwan argues, the role of the state goes far beyond that of the neutral watchman. Over the centuries, government has had to make fundamental decisions about the structure of markets—for instance, in relation to property rights. Here he uses the example of water rights and the effect these have had on agriculture and the development of the mills (which were the first wave of factories in the Industrial Revolution).[12] "To leave things to the market would be to leave things to past intervention."[13] In the words of Elmar Altwater, "A pure market economy has never existed in history; it has always been politically regulated by society. The invisible hand of the market has to be supported by the visible hand of state intervention, and both require the 'third hand' of a network of social and economic institutions."[14]

Polanyi's concern (in *The Great Transformation*) was to show how this has happened with the UK economy. One simple example is the way in which peasants were systematically deprived of their land and forced into the status of wage laborers, so that by the end of the seventeenth century English landlords controlled as much as seventy to seventy-five percent of cultivable land. "As the demand for a growing full-time proletariat increased, so did the pressure to expropriate the land or access to the land of the semi-proletariat."[15] This development of the market economy did not happen naturally, but by force and by government legislation.

The problem is that governments either reflect the interests of the most powerful, or, increasingly, are unable to resist the interests of the most powerful. As Arrighi (followed by Harvey) has argued, there are two different logics of the exercise of hegemonic power—that of territorial rulers and that of the barons of capitalism. Very often these logics act in

11. Ibid., 119.

12. Ibid., 127.

13. Ibid., 131.

14 Altwater, *The Future of the Market*, 238.

15. McNally, *Against the Market*, 18.

collusion. Sometimes they come into conflict with each other.[16] However, it is the argument of Philip Goodchild that, in the last thirty years, since the movement of capital has been deregulated, "it is like gas that has been let out of a bottle . . . states that have released the power of capital have little choice but to subordinate all other political aims to the attraction of investment, or risk losing the source of their power. Money is the supreme political authority in modernity."[17]

To highlight the significance of this reality for the majority of the world's population, we need only look at how this power of money has now enveloped the whole world—even where there is very little of it. When we talk about globalization, what we are referring to is not just the expansion of trading to include the whole world, but a movement in which the whole world is becoming subject to the power of money. It would be possible to argue, in fact, that the extension of trading by the leading economic powers has been consciously aimed at bringing all nations under that power. In the same way as I described this to be true of individuals, so I believe it is true of nations—as soon as you enter trading relationships using money, you become entrapped in a system whose rules have to be kept. Superficially, to receive money for the sale of a commodity may feel like acquiring riches, but that money can only be used in accordance with the rules that govern its use.

In many cases in international trade there is an explicit requirement that money received from the sale of a commodity be used to buy commodities in return from the same country. Where this is not the case, a country may, instead, be in debt arrears that (under present rules) are obliged to be cleared. Add to this the temptation to invest in foreign countries (where interest rates may be higher) and the desire of the population for foreign goods (especially foreign technology), and it is clear that, once you have entered the world's monetary system, you have very little freedom to develop your economy as you might wish. In the words of Daniel Bell, "Humanity is delivered to the capitalist order by means of a vast matrix of technologies of power."[18] Franz Hinkelammert goes so far as to say that since the 1970s capitalism has become a "savage capitalism" that involves an aggressive attack on the power of the nation-state. In this

16. Arrighi, *The Long Twentieth Century*, 33; Harvey, *The New Imperialism*, 27.
17. Goodchild, *Theology of Money*, 62.
18. Bell, *Liberation Theology after the End of History*, 32.

situation the population of the Third World has been rendered largely redundant, and Third World development is no longer perceived as a goal to be attained.[19]

Biblical Perspectives

In earlier discussions on justice I observed how neglect of the Mosaic legislation regarding the care of the poor resulted in the creation of structures of power regarded by the prophets as unjust, and which often resulted in the oppression of the weaker by the stronger. I showed further how Jesus, the New Testament writers, and the church fathers accepted this understanding, and urged on Christians an ethic of solidarity and generosity. In the book of Revelation, however, the conflict is dramatically intensified; the author thinks of earthly events being mirrored by "heavenly" ones, involving an intense warfare. Clearly written in a period of severe persecution, Revelation urges suffering Christians to hold on to their faith, even to the point of death, whatever attempts may be made to force them to compromise. The pictures of "the beast out of the sea" (13:1–10) and the prostitute Babylon (17–18) would have been taken by their first readers as referring to the Roman Empire under whose oppression they were suffering. Accepting that the book is relevant to every century, Rowland identifies "the beast of the sea" (13:1–10) with political dominion, "the beast out of the earth" (13:11–18) with the ideology and ideological institutions that support it, and the prostitute "Babylon" (17–18) with the whole social system supported by the political power.[20]

The "mark of the beast" which was imprinted forcibly on the hand or forehead of everyone, small and great, meant that "no one could buy or sell unless he had the mark" (13:16–17), and the author taunts the merchants of the earth who "grew rich from her excessive luxuries" (18:3) and who will mourn so bitterly when no one buys their cargoes any more (18:11–20)—all of which points to a deep disenchantment with the economic structures of the period. Rowland argues that the famous passage in Romans 13, which argues for obedience to the state, "needs to

---

19. Quoted in Ibid., 10–12.

20. An excellent summary of different interpretations is given in Kovacz and Rowland, *Revelation*, 147–58 and 177–89.

be qualified by the more realistic portrayal of Revelation 13,"[21] where it is revealed that state power can in fact be *demonic*.[22]

The political and economic implications are summarized by Rowland in this way:

> What Revelation refuses to allow is a view of economic and political activity which stresses their autonomy. . . . Acts of trade and commerce and political processes are shown to be shot through with conflicts of interest which are of paramount importance in the concerns of religious people. . . . Revelation, therefore, does not allow a view of society which accepts that it has been secularized and can be understood in its various constituent parts without reference to God. Revelation reminds us that to suppose that there is a 'divine law' which undergirds exchange in the market place, which is not to be troubled by matters of conscience or moral issues, is repugnant to the Christian gospel.[23]

Principalities and Powers

Revelation's reference to heavenly powers like "the beast out of the sea" alerts us to a theme that recurs in different forms throughout the biblical record—namely, that behind all that can be seen there are invisible powers that influence (for good or evil) what happens on the earth. G. B. Caird traced this realization back to the pagan theodicies that are still accepted by many peoples to this very day. What was to be the response of the Israelites to these pagan deities that they encountered? One obvious response, says Caird, would be to identify Yahweh with one or other of the pagan gods. Another would be to deny these deities any reality whatever. The response eventually adopted, however, was to accept their existence, but to assert that they were subject to the supreme authority of Yahweh.[24] This included the powers of nature, the sun, moon and stars, and all the gods recognized by the nations round about. These ideas were developed in later Jewish writing—so that we read in the book of Daniel, for instance, of a war between "the prince of Greece" and "the prince of Persia"

---

21. Rowland, *Revelation*,116.

22. Ibid., 115.

23. Ibid., 135.

24. Caird, *Principalities and Powers*, 1–4.

(Daniel 10:13 and 20), which clearly refers to a conflict, not only between nations, but between the spiritual powers behind them. Throughout the Roman Empire there was widespread acceptance both of the existence of spiritual powers and that each nation had its own particular god acting behind the scenes on its behalf.

The gospel records include many accounts of Jesus's victories over evil spirits and his recognition that behind them lay the power of Satan (e.g., Luke 11:14–22). The whole emphasis, however, is on how this demonstrates the supreme power of God: "If I by the finger of God cast out demons, then the kingdom of God has come to you" (Luke 11:20). St. John makes the broad categorical statement that "the reason the Son of God appeared was to destroy the devil's work" (1 John 3:8).

In the writings of St. Paul are many references to spiritual powers. It is clear that he accepts their existence, though it seems that he saw no reason to spend time differentiating between them. Once again, the great theme is that Christ, particularly through his death on the cross (Colossians 2:15) has won a decisive victory over them. Though evil powers may continue to attack us, the power of Christ is more than sufficient to defeat them (Ephesians 6:10–13; Romans 8:38–39).

The Powers and Money

In *Money and Power*, written in 1950, though not translated into English until 1984, Jacques Ellul explored the language of "the powers" in relation to money. In his use of the term *Mammon*, he argues that Jesus was "not using a rhetorical figure, but pointing to a reality. . . . He is speaking of a power which tries to be like God, which makes itself our master."[25]

Ellul says that money gains its power from the buying-selling relationship, which, he suggests, is gradually involving everything in the world, including human beings. "Human beings . . . are turned away from their true end, their purpose [to glorify God], and at the same time are put under a false authority, one that is not God, whether this is directly or indirectly recognized."[26] He goes so far as to say, in fact, that this subordination occurs in *each selling transaction*, "which inevitably sets up a destructive, competitive relationship, even when the sale is of an ordinary object."[27]

25. Ellul, *Money and Power*, 75–76.

26. Ibid., 78.

27. Ibid., 79.

In addition, Ellul confirms what I have been suggesting when he says that this understanding of the selling relationship "helps us to better understand the whole Hebrew law, which in fact is concerned with protecting human life from the aggression of money."[28] In his Afterword (1979) he says, "All actions and transactions can be explained by the fact that everything has been turned into merchandise. In addition, value is defined as market value, and the first thing we think about in any area is merchandise. . . . The law of merchandise exists wherever money exists. It does not result only from bad use, or from any particular economic structure: *money is implicated by its nature*."[29] In 1950, however, he had been reduced to saying that how money gets its power "is an absurdity which neither economists nor sociologists are able to clarify."[30] He just had to say that it must be traceable to the spiritual power of money.

This is the reason, he says, for the assertion of Jesus that we cannot serve both God and Mammon:

> Do we really believe that if money were only an object with no spiritual significance Jesus would have gone that far? To love money, to be attached to it, is to hate God. We can now understand why St. Paul says that the love of money is the root of all evil. This is not a hackneyed bit of popular morality. It is an accurate summary of this conflict. Insofar as the love of money is hatred for God, it certainly is a root of all the evils that accompany separation from God.[31]

He then goes on to develop the idea of Mammon as "one of the conquered, deposed powers which Christ, by dying on the cross, has stripped of authority . . . but it retains a strength that is greater than ours."[32]

I will return soon to the idea of money as a power. For the moment it is necessary to refer to the major weakness of Ellul's treatment—namely, that he considers the only really effective way of countering the power of money is on the personal level. "The proper response to the poor will not be found in adherence to any group or programme. To try to respond by joining a party, by accepting a programme, by working at an institution, is to refuse responsibility, to escape into the crowds when faced with God's question . . . the only attitude that Christianity can require is personal

28. Ibid., 80.
29. Ibid., 166–67, my italics.
30. Ibid., 81.
31. Ibid., 84.
32. Ibid., 85.

commitment."[33] Is this, as we have seen elsewhere, the characteristic Protestant and evangelical reduction of all social issues to personal morality? Or is it a reaction to the system of communism that he found so unsatisfactory? To do him credit, Ellul is right to say that all systems are subject to corruption by corrupt officials and general human weakness, and that the danger of campaigning and systems is that they can bypass the need for personal commitment. "Of course," he says, "we must do everything possible to relieve misfortune, approaching the poor as if we were speaking to Jesus Christ himself."[34] But it seems that the strength of his doctrine of original sin has made him blind to the possibilities of corporate and state action—and thus to a whole area of countering the power that he sees as so invasive.

I now return to the question of money (or Mammon) as a spiritual power. For those who are skeptical about anything that cannot be seen or touched, this idea may not elicit wide acceptance, but, in this postmodern age, it has suddenly become more credible. Walter Wink has explored the idea of the principalities and powers as constituting a "domination system," which consists of an overarching network of powers, characterized by unjust economic relations and oppressive political relations, which has persisted for at least five thousand years, ever since the rise of the great conquest states of Mesopotamia around 3,000 BC.[35] Wink prefers to think of these powers as impersonal entities and is uncertain whether they have actual metaphysical being. Rather, he feels that they have no existence independent of their material counterparts.[36] Of the reality of their power, however, he has no doubts, and he considers them to rule by means of a number of "delusional assumptions," among which he includes the following:

1. Money is the most important value.

2. The production of material goods is more important than the production of healthy and normal people and of sound human relationships.

3. Property is sacred, and property ownership an absolute right.[37]

---

33. Ibid., 159–60.
34. Ibid., 158.
35. Wink, *The Powers That Be*, 39–40.
36. Ibid., 27–29.
37. Wink, *Engaging the Powers*, 95.

It is not clear whether he regards money as one of the powers, or (more precisely) whether there is a power behind the material counterpart of money (e.g., Mammon). It may be that he regards money as one of the instruments used by the powers to enforce their rule. There has been an ongoing debate as to whether the principalities and powers are spiritual beings or the structures of human society. Markus Barth appears to allow for both, when he says that Paul denotes by them the angelic or demonic beings that reside in the heavens, but suggests that there is a "direct association" of these powers "with structures and institutions of life on earth."[38] For myself, I would accept that the powers to which Paul refers are spiritual beings, but suggest that money, as a human creation, should be regarded rather as a weapon in their arsenal (a cosmic power, but not a personal one). As a human creation, we could, with legitimacy, regard it as an idol. Altogether, when understood in all its ramifications, money has become like a god, requiring human allegiance, bringing human beings into slavery, and frustrating the good purposes that God has for his creation.

Liberation Theology

Potentially the most promising theological attempt to cope with the power of money has been the Liberation Theology first developed in the Roman Catholic Church in Latin America during the late 1960s. The aim of Liberation theologians has always been to see the establishment of an economic order based on the satisfaction of basic needs rather than the domination of capital. To achieve this involves the challenging of the "sinful structures" that characterize the capitalist economy. Unfortunately, according to Valpy Fitzgerald, "A theology of the economy as such has not yet been fully worked out."[39] At the same time, "the orthodox prescriptions of macroeconomic policy have gone largely uncontested except by general denunciations of capitalism."[40] As part of this neglect, there has been little discussion of the nature of money—despite the dominant role ascribed to it by Marx. It has fallen to Franz Hinkelammert, a German resident in Latin America for many years—in his book *The Ideological*

---

38. Barth, *Ephesians*, 1:154.

39. Fitzgerald, "The Economics of Liberation Theology," 225.

40. Ibid., 227.

Weapons of Death—to look more seriously at the question of money and how it might integrate with a theology of liberation.

The first part of Hinkelammert's treatment is to expound Marx's discussion of the fetishism of money and capital, as found in the first book of *Capital*. Beginning (like Adam Smith) with the division of labor as the original seed of capitalism, Marx maintains that, as soon as a commodity enters the market, it develops a life of its own which in various ways controls the person to whom it belongs. Hinkelammert quotes him, saying:

> To find an analogy we must take flight into the misty realm of religion. There the products of the human brain appear as autonomous figures endowed with a life of their own, which enter into relations both with each other and with the human race. So it is in the world of commodities with the products of men's hands.[41]

This Marx calls "the fetishism which attaches itself to the products of labour as soon as they are produced as commodities."[42] Such fetishism becomes more obvious, however, when money comes to act as that by which all commodities are valued. Here Marx says:

> Since money does not reveal what has been transformed into it, everything, commodity or not, is convertible into money. Everything becomes saleable and purchaseable. Circulation becomes the great social retort into which everything is thrown, to come out again as the money crystal. Nothing is immune from this alchemy. . . . Ancient society therefore denounced it as tending to destroy the economic and moral order. Modern society . . . greets gold as its Holy Grail, as the glittering incarnation of its innermost principle of life.[43]

The problem is, for Marx and for Hinkelammert, that money and capital (made up largely of money) can produce a system that can enslave those involved with it. Hinkelammert summarizes Marx by saying, "Capital, living off the life of workers in this manner, threatens them with death. Capital guarantees the life only of those workers necessary for its own life process. It therefore changes into an all-powerful force, capable of pouncing on and battering the worker at any moment."[44]

---

41. Marx, *Capital*, bk. 1, part 1, ch. 1, p. 165.

42. Ibid.

43. Ibid., ch. 3, p. 320.

44. Hinkelammert, *Ideological Weapons of Death*, 30.

Hinkelammert seems to accept all this as a helpful analysis of what is happening under capitalism. In part one, he merely quotes Marx and gives the impression of accepting what he says. But then in part two he starts to develop a Christian theology that reaches much the same conclusions. Beginning with the bodily resurrection of Jesus as a demonstration of the eternal significance of bodily life, he uses the theology of St. Paul to show that God's purposes for Christians, and indeed for the whole world, are concerned with bodily, material life. In opposition are the powers of the law, sin, and death, but the one who has faith in Christ is delivered from their control and starts in this life to experience what will be fully experienced when the world is finally redeemed. "When faith (the law of the Spirit of life) replaces the law, the law of sin and its realm of death are destroyed. In the law of sin the body was in slavery to the flesh. The body is now freed from this slavery. The self of sin and of the flesh is crucified and the body is resurrected for life."[45]

In the realm of sin and death, Hinkelammert argues that Paul gives a particular role to what he calls the "money god." His own translation of Ephesians 5:5 talks of "the greedy, who serve the Money God." He then makes much of 1 Timothy 6:10, which he interprets as saying, "the root of all evil lies in love of money—the money god. Previously the expression of sin was its inclination towards death. Now money is the root of all evil and drags its victims down 'to ruin and destruction.'"[46]

Later Hinkelammert refers to the "supernatural forces of evil" in Ephesians 6:12, of which he assumes money to be one, but regrets that, because of his position in history, Paul was not able to follow his convictions through to an effective praxis:

> He is unable to focus the question around any kind of praxis, simply because he has no adequate concept of the bodily connection uniting human beings. Such a concept would permit him to come to a more specific notion of authority and class structure on the basis of love for neighbour. He cannot use love for neighbour to mediate class structure and authority without such a bodily reference point, which in the last analysis is always the division of labour. Limited by being where he is in history, he cannot discover

45. Ibid., 137.
46. Ibid., 140.

any kind of praxis either. Paul discovers the fetish as Antichrist but the only stance he can take toward it is eschatological.[47]

The relevant praxis for the modern era Hinkelammert regards as that recommended by Liberation theologians. With this in mind, he launches into a condemnation of the characteristic theology of the Catholic Church, which he accuses of departing from the true path when it started to recognize private property as a natural right (in contrast to the teaching of Aquinas, who, while recognizing practical arguments for private property, asserted that the goods of the earth are for the general good). According to Hinkelammert, the insistence that the goods of the earth cannot be claimed absolutely as private property but are essentially for general use strikes at the very root of the capitalist system. Recent unwillingness to accept this view in the Catholic Church may be attributed to its paranoia concerning communism. This paranoia was certainly behind much criticism of Liberation Theology. For Hinkelammert, however, this is the critical point in his philosophy. In his understanding, refusal to accept the premise of the earth's goods serving the common welfare has led to the "anti-utopianism" that has characterized the church from the Middle Ages to the present—a mindset that concentrates on spiritual issues to the neglect of the poor. He summarizes:

> Because life is a real and material life that cannot be replaced by any "true or spiritual life," this is the verdict that must be pronounced over property: a property system is legitimate only insofar as it is compatible with the real material life of all. . . . This duty/right to live may therefore clash with the property system. To the extent that such a clash takes place, there is a duty/right to change it. In the last resort—and only in the last resort—this means the right to use force to carry out that change. . . . If violence is to be avoided, owners must give way. . . . the right to life is never a right to property; it is always the right to real, material life, concrete life.[48]

In other words, Hinkelammert is definitely urging a socialist solution backed up, if necessary, by violence. And it is clear he is thinking not only about land, but of all kinds of property—which, in the contemporary situation, means money.

47. Ibid., 151.
48. Ibid., 263.

A second book, *Property for People, Not for Profit*, which Hinkelammert wrote in partnership with Ulrich Duchrow, traces in much more detail the argument we have just summarized, giving particular emphasis to the part I have already ascribed to John Locke. It is significant (in the light of my interpretation of Mammon) that the writers conclude with recommendations not about property, but about money, and about how its influence can be reduced in the world economy. These include proposals that the share of "debt-money" must be reduced and the share of debt-free money in circulation increased,[49] that real interest should not exceed the added value produced (which implies the political re-regulation of interest rates),[50] the cancellation of debts owed by developing countries (or their replacement by interest-free special drawing rights),[51] the development of alternative bank systems and credit cooperatives,[52] and (in order to counter speculation) a turnover tax on all currency transactions (sometimes known as the "Tobin" tax, after its first proponent).[53] The book closes with the call that Duchrow had been making for some time, and which had been taken up by a number of church bodies: that churches should engage in a *processus confessionis* against global economic injustice and the destruction of nature.[54] Significantly, this chapter is entitled "God or Mammon? A Confessional Issue for the Churches in the Context of Social Movements."[55] The authors understand money/possessions (as I have interpreted Mammon) to be the great alternative power to that of God, and that Christians must take their stand on the side of God.

In his book *The Future of Liberation Theology* (2004), Ivan Petrella argues that Liberation Theology seems to have lost its way following the collapse of the Soviet Union and its satellite states and with the general assumption that socialism has failed to produce the alternative society towards which expectations were built. He attributes this particularly to an obsessional focus on capitalism as a system to be overthrown. According to Petrella, this obsession was based on the "dependency theory" that

49. Duchrow and Hinkelammert, *Property for People, Not for Profit*, 189.

50. Ibid., 191–92.

51. Ibid., 192.

52. Ibid., 193.

53. Ibid.

54. Ibid., 204–24.

55. Ibid., 204.

the poverty and powerlessness experienced in Latin America were all the result of the oppression and domination of Western powers. To some extent theologians were beginning to see the inadequacy of this theory, but, still regarding capitalism as a monolithic whole, had not analyzed it sufficiently to discern what aspects of capitalism are particularly problematic. In his words:

> The best way to combat the idolatrous nature of capitalism . . . is to rid it of its systemic, all powerful, all encompassing, quasi-divine quality. The task is to show that the idol is an idol; that it is made of clay. Only then can room be made for the development of new historical projects.[56]

In my submission, to "show" that capitalism is idolatrous can only be achieved through a much more detailed analysis than Liberation theologians have been able to do. It is the claim of this book that such a project needs to begin with an analysis of the role of money in the capitalist system, especially in its "free-market" form. Having done this, I suggest that it will not be sufficient simply to replace a blanket condemnation of capitalism with a blanket condemnation of money. Rather it will require explanation of how money has become an idol, and precisely how it produces oppression. Only after that it will be possible to consider suitable praxis.

Engaging the Power of Money

I have listed some of the strategies recommended by Duchrow and Hinkelammert for dealing with the power of money. Similar suggestions have been made by other writers. What these proposals have in common is that they tend to tackle the symptoms rather than the roots of money's power. An alternative strategy has been to marginalize money—by creating new kinds of money separate from the dominant economy, or just by operating without any money at all. The problem with creating new kinds of money, however, is that they may ultimately come to produce the same negative effects as existing forms of money. And, even if there is no commodity called money, there will always be (as shown in chapter 1) a money of account. In general terms, I would urge that a more effective solution would be to cut the roots of money's power in some of the ways

56. Petrella, *The Future of Liberation Theology*, 85.

suggested in the various sections of this thesis (e.g., by regulating debt and tackling the question of interest).

What cannot be overlooked is that money is never money *by itself*. It always *belongs to somebody*—the chief possessors being governments, banks, and large corporations. This being the case, engaging the power of money will inevitably involve conflict with the chief owners of money—together with those who create money (creators of money) and those who decide the rules by which it is to be used (legitimators of money). Wink envisages a great global struggle against invisible powers, and he places enormous stress on the weapon of nonviolence. While not disputing this vision, I would emphasize the practical reality that the chief owners of money, the creators of money and the legitimators of money are a formidable force who will be very reluctant to relinquish their power. If the realities of the power of money could be properly explained, it is possible that a grassroots revolution could be stimulated. There are certainly many in the Christian tradition who place their hopes in the formation of grassroots alternative societies, and it could be argued that this is what the Christians of the New Testament period were trying to create. There are some indications of greater understanding among politicians of the power of money as a result of the recent economic crisis. On the other hand, there are also signs that few lessons have actually been learned, and it may take a far more severe crisis (which could well occur) to enable them to face up to the fundamental weaknesses of our present system. In this respect, perhaps we may have to face the kind of "battle" envisaged by the book of Revelation. The conviction asserted by that book, however, is that, whatever powers are raised against him, God is greater than them all.

Decoding Mammon

As I HAVE BEEN looking at money from various viewpoints, it has been against the background that, for most people, money is a useful commodity that has enabled fruitful exchange of resources and a growth in the world economy that has produced increased well-being for millions of people. Equally significantly, perhaps, it has been against the background of a dominant political theory that this growth and prosperity are best achieved by allowing markets (that is, money) to operate freely without restrictions. This theory has been dominant now for thirty years, though there has been a realization that some restrictions may be necessary, in order to control some of the more extreme fluctuations of the market. There is, as a result of the economic crisis that emerged in 2007, a feeling in many quarters that such restrictions may need to be strengthened if the crisis is to be brought to an end. For the great majority of Western governments, businesses and economists, however, there remains a general consensus that money should continue to be allowed to function as freely as possible. To some extent this may be the product of self-interest. It may also be the result of uncertainty or even fear about the effects that significant change might produce.

In the discipline of Christian theology, for several centuries a generally positive view of money as an institution has prevailed. It could be said that there has always been an appreciation of the dangers produced by love of money. Money itself, however, especially since the Enlightenment, has been seen as neutral or positive in its effects. The chief periods when there has been suspicion about it have been the medieval scholastic period and (among a few writers) the past twenty years. But even now many still see things in the same way as governments, businesses, and economists—possibly because they haven't considered sufficiently the kind of arguments adduced in this book. I repeat that my argument is not to dispute the usefulness of money or the many achievements that it has made possible. Rather, it is to suggest that, along with the usefulness of money and its many achievements, there are many negative effects—and that these effects can be discovered by a more careful survey and use of Christian theology.

I have entitled this book *Decoding Mammon*. In general terms, it could be said the whole purpose of the book has been to discover the reasons why Jesus was so suspicious of it. Nearing the end of this study, it should now be possible to see more clearly why this was, and to decode more precisely what mammon actually is.

I have already suggested in the introduction that mammon, at the time of Jesus, referred to all material possessions (whatever form they might take). Even the rich probably possessed little in terms of gold or silver. Most were rich because of the land or houses that they possessed. All of this, however, could be changed into money, and the money used for whatever purposes they wished. Those who were poor, in the same way, were those who possessed little or nothing in terms of land and houses—and, therefore, little that could be changed into money. It was on this basis that I felt justified in considering the writings of the church fathers on the subject of property. In our day, by way of contrast, people possess a much greater proportion of their possessions in terms of money. Even what they hold in other forms can be valued and realized in terms of money. I have accepted, therefore, that in our day it is perfectly justifiable to apply Jesus's words about mammon to money (as it is, in fact, translated in a number of modern Bible translations).

I return, however, to the questions raised by the fact that Matthew and Luke made no attempt to translate the Aramaic "mammon" into Greek. I suggested in the introduction that one of the reasons may have been the difficulty of finding a Greek word that was an adequate translation. In the chapter on the nature of money, however, I underlined the extraordinary complexity of money, and that it certainly cannot be regarded as a commodity like any other commodity. This being the case, it could well be that it was some appreciation of this fact that prevented a translation that might have identified money as a commodity (silver or gold or whatever). In other words, it could well be that Jesus, Matthew, and Luke all saw wealth (even if sometimes held in the form of a commodity called money) as something much more than a commodity and more like the deceptive power that I have been suggesting money to be. The arguments presented by sociologists like Simmel have concentrated far more on the role that money plays than on that of which it may consist, and on the social relationships that it expresses. My own studies in the Christian tradition, revealing the numerous negative values that money encapsulates, have suggested that we need to regard it as a cosmic power, in the language used in the New Testament and in writers like Ellul, Hinkelammert, and Wink.

The argument presented here has been a cumulative one. In the first chapter we saw that it makes less and less sense to regard money as a commodity, in that it rarely exists nowadays in material form and is so easily created "out of nothing" by governments and banks. In this respect, money can be expanded enormously (theoretically to infinity). But this leads very quickly to instability, speculation, the overvaluation of money-trading in relation to productive activity, and eventually to the exhaustion of the resources of the planet. The scholastics (following Aristotle) were opposed to the creation of money out of nothing (in the form of interest-bearing credit). In recent years virtually all money is created in the form of credit, and I have argued that it bears little relation to the wealth of the "real" economy, being used much of the time for speculative activity rather than for improving the life of society.

In relation to money as credit and debt, I have shown that (for all its value in helping people out of difficult situations and in generating new productive opportunities), it carries the danger of debts getting out of hand, so that they cannot be repaid, of the poor being reduced to hopelessness, and of debt being used to further economic growth regardless of any negative effects. Here the Old Testament Torah legislates explicitly for the cancellation of all debts after seven years—so that, even if theologians don't argue today for cancellation in such a short period, there is a clear presumption in Christian theology that debt is dangerous and may sometimes need to be cancelled, that it should certainly be reduced, and needs urgently to be brought under control. The use of credit to finance commercial activity has now reached such an extent that it places many organizations and individuals in perilous situations, and the danger of a general financial collapse is never far away.

In relation to money as interest, I drew attention to the side effects of interest conveniently listed by Paul Mills: the unjust and destabilizing allocation of returns between the users and suppliers of finance, the misallocation of finance to the safest borrowers rather than to the most productive, a propensity to finance speculation in assets and property, an inherently unstable banking system, a short-termist investment strategy, a concentration of financial wealth in fewer and fewer hands, and a rapid flow of financial capital across regions and countries. I also referred to the real danger of producing inflation. I drew attention to how the necessity of paying interest (especially compound interest) can whittle away the resources of the poor, and how the making of profits in order to enable the payment of interest leads inexorably to unnecessary economic activity, to speculation, and to the depletion of the planet's resources. In this area, although it allows interest payments to be made on loans to foreigners, the Torah forbids the charging of interest to a fellow Israelite. The scholastics, following Aristotle and their understanding of natural law, opposed interest payments in principle, making as few exceptions as they could. This opposition has continued in Roman Catholic theology and is being increasingly appreciated by writers in other traditions.

In relation to the question of justice, I have shown how the introduction of money has led to an individualistic attitude to life, to great inequalities between rich and poor, and to a seeking for profit out of others rather than seeking their benefit. In contrast, the Scriptures and the majority of both Jewish and Christian thinkers have always insisted that moral considerations should take precedence over financial ones, that care for the poor should always be the highest priority, that the interests of the community matter more than those of the individual, and that property (including money) should be used for the benefit of all, rather than being the exclusive possession of individuals. In an economy that allows money free rein, this means public regulation and direction so that money is shared on the basis of justice.

In relation to the question of value, I indicated how giving monetary values to items, based on the prices they can obtain in the market, may bear no relation to their usefulness in the community, and has led gradually to the dominance of money values. At the same time, there are many things that cannot be valued in money terms, but which may be far more important than those that are. In this vein, the Bible and Christian theology continually emphasize values like solidarity, mercy, justice, health, and care for the planet, and they urge that value be measured in moral terms. I mentioned a number of suggestions that have been made as to how monetary values could approach more closely to social value, but this is an area requiring much research.

In relation to desire, I underlined what many others have described: how the fact that money can buy (almost) everything leads to money being the most desirable item in the world and to the putting of its acquisition before every other consideration. On the other hand, the Christian tradition teaches that we should resist that temptation and desire ends like goodness, love, and the benefit of others, trusting God to meet our needs through his love and generosity. What is clear is that our present capitalist society promotes selfish desire, and (from Adam Smith to the neoliberals of today) almost justifies it. I have suggested, therefore, that the remedy required is not just a change of attitude in individuals, but radical changes to the system as a whole, so that the appeal to desire has less prominence, and the system is geared far more to human needs and the sustainability of the creation.

In the critical chapter on power, I have described how every money transaction involves a power relationship and is distorted by unequal power relationships to the advantage of the powerful and the disadvantage of the weak. In this way, money becomes the dominant power in the world, and the interests of the weak and vulnerable are increasingly marginalized. I further underlined the biblical teaching about cosmic powers and the identification of money by Ellul, Wink, and Hinkelammert as either a cosmic power or else an instrument of cosmic powers. For those who have difficulty in accepting the existence of such powers, I suggest that it must be clear, nevertheless, since money has been deregulated, that it holds everybody in a grip from which it is virtually impossible to escape. The Bible and Christian tradition, on the other hand, insist that supreme authority belongs to God, that he must be served before anyone or anything else, and that his priorities are the interests of the poor and vulnerable. In our present situation, this would seem to require (at the very least) strong public regulation, especially to counter the unequal power relationships involved in money transactions and where an individual faces the power of banks and large corporations, together with those who establish the rules under which money is used.

In general terms, it could be said that money (if not restricted in any way) favors the individual over against the community, the rich over against the poor, the self over against other people, economic growth over against the environment, and the material over against the spiritual (or immaterial). In this last respect, Jesus urges, "Do not store up for your-selves treasures on earth, where moth and rust destroy, and where thieves break in and steal. But store up for yourselves treasures in heaven, where moth and rust do not destroy, and thieves do not break in and steal. For where your treasure is, there your heart will be also" (Matthew 6:19–21).

Money has great uses, but these numerous disadvantages demon-strate (in opposition to the current philosophy of free markets) that it needs to be used within strict limits designed to reduce these disadvan-tages to a minimum. If such limits cannot be established at the national level, then they need to be established internationally. The alternative of not using money at all I take to be both unrealistic and unnecessary. Much more fruitful, in the long run, would be creating money whose value was determined by social considerations rather than by market conditions. Tackling the problem from the grassroots upwards by establishing zones with their own independent currencies may be a realistic possibility, but the effects of this tactic on the system as a whole could be very slow and (considering the immensity of the problem) too late. Local currencies may not be subject to as many disadvantages as national ones, but will still need to be watched carefully so that they do not develop the problems inextricably involved with all money.

Some of the more radical solutions may take time (and a lot of mo-tivation) to be realized. In the long run they may well be unavoidable. My own conviction, however, bearing in mind the need for urgent action and trying to be realistic about what can actually be achieved, is simply to turn away from the doctrine of free markets that has ruled for too long, and to accept the necessity of much stronger and more extensive regulation of money in all aspects of the economy.

Ultimately, what we are facing is that money is a human construct, and that those who have constructed it are fallible, fallen creatures. Money is not something "natural" that has always existed. It is not a perfect con-struction, but one constructed over millennia to suit the interests of those in power. The Archbishop of Canterbury, in a recent book, rightly asserts that "regulation alone is ill equipped to solve our problems." He says, "The issues need to be internalized in terms of the sort of life that humans might find actively desirable and admirable, the sort of biographies that carry conviction by their self-consistency." And this, he says, means re-covering "the language of the virtues," which has virtually disappeared in our day.[1] If this could be achieved, it would certainly make a great deal of difference, and it is the role of Christian preachers to argue that, in Christ, this kind of transformation is possible. However, this book claims that a system has now been developed from whose clutches it is very difficult to escape. As suggested earlier, it may be that only a complete breakdown of the present system will persuade people that truly radical action is necessary. The recent crisis has certainly dented confidence in the present system, but, unfortunately, the rescue operation mounted has only succeeded in landing us with an even greater burden of debt than that which caused the crisis, and there is little sign of urgency in dealing with the sort of issues we have highlighted here.

This may sound excessively pessimistic, but the heart of this study has been to demonstrate that our problems stem, not simply from human failings, but from the nature of money itself. As St. Paul asserted that "our struggle is not against flesh and blood, but against the authorities, against the powers of this dark world and against the spiritual forces of evil in the heavenly realms" (Ephesians 6:12), so I would argue that we are dealing here not so much with human weakness as with a cosmic power that exercises its influence at every level throughout the whole world—so that Jesus was totally justified in regarding it as *the* great rival to God. If the problems posed by the very existence of money are not tackled seriously, it could dissolve the whole fabric of our society—through the poverty and death of millions of underprivileged people, through the bankruptcy of many states, and through the increasing destruction of the environment. My argument holds that the one solution that could solve our problem would be to subject the whole system to the lordship of God instead of the lordship of money. Curiously, in a secular world, the starting point of redemption might be to take seriously the insights of Christian theology.

1. Williams, "Knowing Our Limits," 29.

Bibliography

Altwater, Elmar. *The Future of the Market*. English translation by Patrick Camiller. London: Verso, 1993.

Aquinas, Thomas. *The De Malo of Thomas Aquinas*. English ed., edited by Brian Davies. London: Oxford University Press, 2001.

———. *Summa Theologica*. Literally translated by the Fathers of the English Dominican Province. London: Burns Oates & Washbourne, 1920–1929.

Aristotle. *Nichomachean Ethics*. English translation with commentary by Hippocrates G. Apostle. Grinnel, IA: The Peripatetic Press, 1984.

———. *On the Soul*. English translation by Hugh Lawson-Tancred. London: Penguin, 1987.

———. *Politics*. English translation by T. A. Sinclair. London: Penguin, 1962.

Arrighi, Giovanni. *The Long Twentieth Century*. London and New York: Verso, 1994.

Atherton, John. *Christianity and the Market*. London: SPCK, 1992.

Avila, Charles. *Ownership: Early Christian Teaching*. Maryknoll, NY: Orbis, 1983.

Bahro, Rudolf. *Avoiding Social and Ecological Disaster: The Politics of World Transformation*. Bath: Gateway Press, 1994.

Barth, Markus. *Ephesians: A New Translation with Introduction and Commentary*. 2 vols. Anchor Bible. Garden City, NY: Doubleday, 1974.

Bell, Daniel M., Jr. *Liberation Theology after the End of History*. London and New York: Routledge, 2001.

Benedict XIV. *Vix Pervenit*. 1745. Online: http://www.papalencyclicals.net.

Benedict XVI. *Caritas in Veritate*. English translation. Dublin: Veritas Publications, 2009.

Biggar, Nigel. "God in Public Reason." *Studies in Christian Ethics* 19 (2006) 9–19.

Birch, Bruce C. *Let Justice Roll Down*. Louisville: Westminster John Knox, 1991.

Bright, John. *A History of Israel*. London: SCM Press, 1960.

Brueggemann, Walter. *The Prophetic Imagination*. Minneapolis: Fortress, 2001.

———. *Theology of the Old Testament*. Minneapolis: Fortress, 1997.

Buchan, James. *Frozen Desire*. London and Basingstoke: Picador, 1997.

Burnet, Richard, and John Cavanagh. "Electronic Money and the Casino Economy." In *The Case Against the Global Economy: And for a Turn Toward Localization*, edited by Edward Goldsmith and Jerry Mander. London: Earthscan Publications, 2001.

Caird, G. B. *Principalities and Powers*. London: Oxford University Press, 1956.

Calvin, John. *Commentary on the Psalms*. Grand Rapids: Christian Classics Ethereal Library. Online: www.ccel.org.

———. *Harmony of the Law*. Grand Rapids: Christian Classics Ethereal Library. Online: www.ccel.org.

———. *Institutes of the Christian Religion*. London: SCM Press, 1961.

Bibliography

------. *John Calvin's Ecclesiastical Advice*. Translated by Mary Beaty and Benjamin W. Farley. Edinburgh: T&T Clark, 1991.

------. *Sermons on Deuteronomy*. Edinburgh: Banner of Truth Trust, 1987.

Chilton, Bruce. *The Kingdom of God and the Teaching of Jesus*. London: SPCK, 1984.

Chown, John F. *A History of Money from AD 800*. London: Routledge and the Institute of Economic Affairs, 1994.

Cowley, Catherine. *The Value of Money: Ethics and the World of Finance*. London and New York: T&T Clark International, 2006.

Craig, Robert. *Social Concern in the Thought of William Temple*. London: Victor Gollancz, 1963.

Daly, Herman, and John Cobb Jr. *Beyond Growth: The Economics of Sustainable Development*. Boston: Beacon Press, 1996.

------. *The Common Good*. Boston: Beacon Press, 1989.

Davies, Glyn. *A History of Money*. Cardiff: University of Wales Press, 1994.

Davies, W. D., and Allison, D. C., Jr. *A Critical and Exegetical Commentary on the Gospel according to Matthew*. Volume 1: *Introduction and Commentary on Matthew I–VII*. International Critical Commentary. Edinburgh: T. & T. Clark, 1988.

Derrett, J. D. M. *Law in the New Testament*. London: Dartman, Longman & Todd, 1970.

Diwany, Tarek El. *The Problem with Interest*. London: Kreatoc, 2003.

Doctrine Commission of the Church of England. *Being Human: A Christian Understanding of Personhood, Illustrated with Reference to Power, Money, Sex and Time*. London: Church House Press, 2003.

Douglas, Clifford. *Social Credit*. London: Eyre & Spottiswood, 1934.

Dodd, C. H. *The Parables of Jesus*. London: Nisbet & Co., 1935.

Dodd, Nigel. *The Sociology of Money: Economics, Reason and Contemporary Society*. Cambridge: Polity Press, 1994.

Douthwaite, Richard. *The Ecology of Money*. Dartington: Green Books, 1999.

Duchrow, Ulrich. *Alternatives to Global Capitalism*. Utrecht: International Books, 1998.

Duchrow, Ulrich, and Franz Hinkelammert. *Property for People, Not for Profit: Alternatives to the Global Tyranny of Capital*. Geneva: WCC Publications, 2004.

Ellul, Jacques. *Money and Power*. Translated by L. Neff. Downers Grove, IL: InterVarsity Press, 1984.

Faith in the City. By the Archbishop of Canterbury's Commission on Urban Priority Areas. London: Church House Publishing, 1985.

Ferguson, Everett. *Backgrounds of Early Christianity*. Grand Rapids: Eerdmans, 1987.

"Fifth Lateran Council." In *Decrees of the Ecumenical Councils*, edited by Norman P. Tanner, vol. 1. Georgetown: Georgetown University Press, 1990.

Fitzgerald, Valpy. "The Economics of Liberation Theology." In *Cambridge Companion to Liberation Theology*, edited by Christopher Rowland, 218–34. Cambridge: Cambridge University Press, 1999.

Foucault, Michel. "The Subject and Power." In *Power* (The Essential Works of Foucault, 1954–1984, vol. 3), edited by James D. Faubion, translated by Robert Hurley. London: Penguin, 1994.

France, R. T. "God and Mammon." *Evangelical Quarterly* 51 (1979) 3–21.

Friedman, Milton. *Capitalism and Freedom*. Chicago: University of Chicago Press, 1962.

Galbraith, John Kenneth. *The Affluent Society*. London: Penguin, 1987.

------. *A History of Economics*. London: Penguin, 1989.

------. *Money*. London: Andre Deutsch, 1975.

Gay, Craig. *Cash Values*. Grand Rapids: Eerdmans, 2003.

Geldenhuys, J. Norval. *Commentary on the Gospel of Luke*. London: Marshall, Morgan & Scott, 1950.

Glasser, Ralph. *The New High Priesthood*. London: Macmillan, 1967.

Goacher, David. *The Monetary and Financial System*. London Bankers Books, 1993.

Goddard, Andrew. "*Semper Reformanda* in a Changing World: Calvin, Usury and Moral Theology." In *Alister E. McGrath and Evangelical Theology: A Dynamic Engagement*, edited by Sung Wook. Carlisle: Paternoster, 2000.

Goodchild, Philip. *Capitalism and Religion: The Price of Piety*. London and New York: Routledge, 2002.

———. *Theology of Money*. London: SCM Press, 2007.

Gorringe, T. J. "Can Bankers Be Saved?" *Studies in Christian Ethics* 144 (2001) 17–33.

———. *Capital and the Kingdom*. Maryknoll, NY: Orbis, 1994.

———. *The Education of Desire*. London, SCM Press, 2001.

Gottwald, Norman. *The Tribes of Judah*. London: SCM Press, 1980.

Grayston, Kenneth. "Desire." In *A Theological Wordbook of the Bible*, edited by Alan Richardson. London: SCM Press, 1957.

Greco, Thomas H., Jr. *The End of Money and the Future of Civilization*. White River Junction, VT: Chelsea Green Publishing, 2009.

Green, Stephen. *Serving God? Serving Mammon?* London: Marshall Pickering, 1986.

Griffiths, Brian. *The Creation of Wealth*. London: Hodder & Stoughton, 1984.

———. *Morality and the Market Place*. London: Hodder & Stoughton, 1982.

Guthrie, Donald. *The Pastoral Epistles*. Exeter: Paternoster, 1957.

Gutiérrez, Gustavo. *A Theology of Liberation*. London: SCM Press, 1987.

Hanson, Kenneth C., and Douglas E. Oakman: *Palestine in the Time of Jesus: Social Structures and Social Conflicts*. Minneapolis: Fortress, 1998.

Harvey, David. *The New Imperialism*. London: Oxford University Press, 2003.

Hauck, F. "Mamonas." In *Theological Dictionary of the New Testament*, edited by Gerhard Kittel and Gerhard Friedrich, translated by Geoffrey W. Bromiley, 4:388–90. Grand Rapids: Eerdmans, 1968.

Hauerwas, Stanley. "In Praise of *Centesimus Annus*." *Theology* 95 (1992) 416–32.

Hayek, Friedrich. *The Denationalization of Money*. London: Institute of Economic Affairs, 1976.

———. *The Mirage of Social Justice*. Vol. 2 of *Law, Legislation and Liberty*. London and Henley: Routledge & Kegan Paul, 1976.

———. *The Road to Serfdom*. London: Routledge & Kegan Paul, 1948.

Headlam, Stewart. *Christian Socialism*. London: Fabian Society, 1892.

Hengel, Martin. *Property and Riches in the Early Church*. London: SCM Press, 1985.

Herodotus. *The Histories*. Edited by Carolyn Dewald. Translated by Robin Waterfield. London: Oxford University Press, 2008.

Herzog, William R., II. *Parables as Subversive Speech*. Louisville: Westminster/John Knox Press, 1994.

Higginson, Richard. *Called To Account*. Guildford : Eagle, 1993.

———, Michael Parsons, and David Clough (for the Church Investors' Group). *Usury, Investment and the Sub-Prime Sector*. London : Church House Publishing, 2008.

Hilton, Boyd. *The Age of Atonement*. London: Oxford University Press, 1988.

Hinkelammert, Franz. *The Ideological Weapons of Death*. Maryknoll, NY: Orbis, 1986.

Hobbes, Thomas. *Leviathan*. Cambridge: Cambridge University Press, 1996.

Hooft, W. A. Visser 't, and J. H. Oldham. *The Church and Its Function in Society*. London: George Allen & Unwin, 1937.

Hudson, Michael. *The Lost Tradition of Debt Cancellations*. New York: Henry George School of Social Science, 1993.

Hutchinson, Frances, and Brian Burkitt. *The Political Economy of Social Credit and Guild Socialism*. Charlbury, Oxfordshire: Jon Carpenter Publishing, 2005.

Ingham, Geoffrey. *The Nature of Money*. Cambridge: Polity Press, 2004.

Iremonger, F. A. *William Temple*. London: Oxford University Press, 1948.

Jackson, Kevin. *The Oxford Book of Money*. Oxford: Oxford University Press, 1996.

Jackson, Tim. *Prosperity Without Growth: Economics for a Finite Planet*. London: Earthscan, 2009.

Jebb, Sir R. *Sophocles, The Plays and Fragments*. Cambridge: Cambridge University Press, 1928.

Jenkins, David. *Market Whys and Human Wherefores*. London and New York: Continuum, 2000.

John XXIII. *Pacem in Terris*. 1963. In *Catholic Social Thought: The Documentary Heritage*, edited by David O'Brien and Thomas A. Shannon. Maryknoll, NY: Orbis, 2005.

Jolovicz, H. F., and Barry Nichols. *Historical Introduction to the Study of Roman Law*. Cambridge: Cambridge University Press, 1972.

Josephus, Flavius. *Complete Works*. Translated by William Whiston. London: Pickering and Inglis, 1960.

Kelly, J. N. D. *A Commentary on the Pastoral Epistles*. London: Adam and Charles Black, 1973.

Kelly, Patrick Hyde. *Locke on Money*. 2 vols. Oxford: Clarendon, 1991.

Kennedy, Margrit. *Interest and Inflation-Free Money*. Steyerberg: Permakultur Publikationem, 1990.

Keynes, John Maynard. *General Theory of Employment, Interest and Money*. London: Macmillan, 1936.

King, Mervyn. "Challenges for Monetary Policy: New and Old." *Bank of England Quarterly Bulletin* 35 (1999) 397–415.

Knight, George W. *The Pastoral Epistles*. Carlisle: Paternoster, 1992.

Kovacz, Judith, and Christopher Rowland. *Revelation*. Oxford: Blackwell, 2004.

Küng, Hans. *Yes to a Global Ethic*. London: SCM Press, 1995.

Langholm, Odd. *Economics in the Medieval Schools*. Leiden: E.J. Brill, 1992.

Leo XIII. *Rerum Novarum*. 1891. In *Catholic Social Thought: The Documentary Heritage*, edited by David O'Brien and Thomas A. Shannon. Maryknoll, NY: Orbis, 2005.

Linden, Ian. "Globalization and the Church: An Overview." In *Development Matters*, edited by Charles Reed. London: Church House Publishing, 2001.

Little, Lester. *Religious Poverty and the Profit Economy in Medieval Europe*. London: Paul Elek, 1978.

Locke, John. *Two Treatises of Government*. Edited by Peter Laslett. Cambridge: Cambridge University Press, 1994.

Luther, Martin. *Works*. Edited by Walter I. Brant. Philadelphia: Muhlenberg, 1962.

MacEwan, Arthur. *Neo-Liberalism or Democracy?* London and New York: Zed Books, 1999.

MacIntyre, Alasdair. *After Virtue*. Notre Dame, IN: University of Notre Dame Press, 1984.

Mandeville, Bernard. "The Fable of the Bees; or Private Vices Turned to Public Benefits" [1714]. In *Collected Works*. Hildesheim and New York: George Olms Verlag, 1981.

Marx, Karl. *Capital*. Vol. 1: *A Critique of Political Economy*. Translated by Ben Fowkes. London: Penguin, 1976.

———. "The Power of Money in Bourgeois Society." In *Economic and Philosophical Manuscripts of 1844*. Edited and with an introduction by Dirk J. Struik. Translated by Martin Milligan. London: Lawrence & Wishart, 1970.

Marx, Karl, and Friedrich Engels. *The Communist Manifesto*. Edited by D. McLellan. London: Oxford University Press, 1992.

Matera, Frank J. *New Testament Ethics*. Louisville: Westminster John Knox, 1996.

Maurice, F. D. *The Kingdom of Christ*. 2 vols. London: SCM Press, 1958.

McKendrick, Neil, John Brewer, and J. H. Plumb. *The Birth of a Consumer Society*. London: Europa Publications, 1982.

McMurty, John. *The Cancer Stage of Capitalism*. London: Pluto Press, 1999.

McNally, David. *Against the Market*. London and New York: Verso/Left Books, 1994.

Meeks, D. *God the Economist*. Minneapolis: Fortress, 1989.

Migne, Jacques Paul. *Patrologia Graeca*. London: Heinemann, 1953.

———. *Patrologia Latina*. New Jersey: Ridgewood, 1965.

Mills, Paul. *The Ban on Interest: Dead Letter or Radical Solution?* Cambridge: Jubilee Centre, 1993.

———. "The Economy." In *Jubilee Manifesto*, edited by Michael Schluter and John Ashcroft. Cambridge: Jubilee Centre, 2005.

———. *Interest in Interest: The Old Testament Ban on Interest and Its Implications for Today*. Cambridge: Jubilee Centre, 1989.

———. "Should Interest Exist? Non-usurious Finance in Economic Thought, Theory and Practice." Thesis, University of Cambridge, 1994.

Mills, Paul, and John R. Presley. *Islamic Finance: Theory and Practice*. Basingstoke: Macmillan, 1999.

Milton, John. *Paradise Lost*. London: Oxford University Press, 2008.

Mooney, S. C. *Usury, Destroyer of Nations*. Warsaw, OH: Theopolis, 1988.

Myers, Ched. *Binding the Strong Man*. Maryknoll, NY: Orbis. 1988.

Nelson, Benjamin. *The Idea of Usury*. Chicago: University of Chicago Press, 1969.

Nestle, E. "Mammon." In *Encyclopaedia Biblica*, edited by Thomas Kelly Cheyne and John Sutherland Black, 3:2914–15. London: Macmillan, 1902.

New Economics Foundation. *The Great Transition*. London, 2009.

Niebuhr, Reinhold. *Moral Man and Immoral Society*. London: SCM Press, 1963.

Nineham, D. E. *The Gospel of Mark*. London: Penguin, 1977.

Noonan, John. *The Scholastic Analysis of Usury*. Boston: Harvard University Press, 1957.

Norman, Edward. *Church and Society in England, 1770–1970*. London: Oxford University Press, 1976.

Novak, Michael. *The Catholic Ethic and the Spirit of Capitalism*. New York: Free Press, 1993.

———. *The Spirit of Democratic Capitalism*. London: The IEA Health and Social Unit, 1991.

Nussbaum, David. "Does Shareholder Value Drive the World?" In *Christianity and the Culture of Economics*, edited by Donald Hay and Alan Kreider. Cardiff: University of Wales, 2001.

O'Brien, David, and Thomas A. Shannon, eds. *Catholic Social Thought: The Documentary Heritage*. Maryknoll, NY: Orbis, 2005.

Bibliography

O'Connor, June. "Making a Case for the Common Good in a Global Society—The United Nations Human Development Reports 1990–(2001)." *Journal of Religious Ethics* 30 (2002) 157–73.

Petrella, Ivan. *The Future of Liberation Theology.* Aldershot: Ashgate, 2004.

Pettifor, Ann. *The Coming First World Debt Crisis.* Basingstoke: Palgrave Macmillan, 2006.

Phan, Peter. *Social Thought.* Message of the Fathers of the Church 20. Wilmington, DE: Michael Glazier, 1984.

Polanyi, Karl. *The Great Transformation.* London: Victor Gollancz, 1946.

Preston, Ronald. *Church and Society in the Late Twentieth Century: The Economic and Political Task.* London: SCM Press, 1983.

———. *Religion and the Persistence of Capitalism.* London: SCM Press, 1979.

Rad, Gerhard von. *Old Testament Theology.* 2 vols. Edinburgh: Oliver & Boyd, 1962–1965.

Rieger, Joerg. *No Rising Tide: Theology, Economics, and the Future.* Minneapolis: Fortress, 2009.

Robertson, James. *Future Wealth: A New Economics for the 21st. Century.* London: Cassel, 1990.

Roman Catholic Church. *Code of Canon Law* [English translation of *Codex Iuris Canonici*]. London: Collins, 1983.

Rowbotham, Michael. *The Grip of Death.* Charlbury, Oxfordshire: Jon Carpenter, 1998.

Rowland, Christopher. *Revelation.* London: Epworth Press, 1993.

Russell, D. S. *Between the Testaments.* London: SCM Press, 1960.

Salins, Antoine de, and Francois de Galhan. *The Modern Development of Financial Activities in the Light of the Ethical Demands of Christianity.* English edition. Vatican City: Pontifical Council for Justice and Peace (Libreria Editrice Vaticana), 1994.

Schmidt, Thomas. *Hostility to Wealth in the Synoptic Gospels.* Sheffield: Sheffield Academic Press, 1987.

Schumacher, E. F. *Small Is Beautiful.* London: Sphere Books, 1974.

Seaford, Richard. *Money and the Early Greek Mind.* Cambridge: Cambridge University Press, 2004.

Selby, Peter. *Grace and Mortgage.* London: Dartman, Longman & Todd, 1997.

Shakespeare, William. *The Merchant of Venice.* London: Oxford University Press, 2008.

Simmel, Georg. *The Philosophy of Money.* English translation by Tom Bottomore and David Frisby. London: Routledge & Kegan Paul, 1990.

Smith, Adam. *The Wealth of Nations.* London: Penguin, 1970 and 1999.

Spencer Nick. *The Measure of All Things?* Cambridge: Jubilee Centre, 2003.

Stiglitz, Joseph. *Globalization and Its Discontents.* London: Penguin, 2002.

Stiltner, Brian. *Religion and the Common Good: Catholic Contributions to Building Community in a Liberal Society.* Lanham, MD: Rowman & Littlefield, 1999.

Sung, Jung Mo. *Desire, Market and Religion.* London: SCM Press, 2007.

Tanner, Kathryn. *Economy of Grace.* Minneapolis: Fortress, 2005.

Tanner, Norman P. *Decrees of the Ecumenical Councils.* London: Sheed & Ward and Georgetown University Press, 1990.

Tawney, R. H.. *The Acquisitive Society.* London: Wheatsheaf Books, 1982.

———. *Religion and the Rise of Capitalism.* London: Penguin, 1938.

Temple, William. *Christianity and the Social Order.* London: Penguin, 1942.

———. *The Church Looks Forward.* London: Macmillan, 1944.

Troeltsch, Ernst. *The Social Teaching of the Christian Churches.* Translated by Olive Wyon. New York: Macmillan, 1931.

Veblen, Thomas. *The Theory of the Leisure Class*. London: George Allen & Unwin, 1925.

Waterman, A. M. C. *Political Economy and Christian Theology since the Enlightenment*. Basingstoke: Palgrave Macmillan, 2004.

Weber, Max. *The Protestant Ethic and the Spirit of Capitalism*. Translated by Talcott Parsons. London: George Allen and Unwin, 1978.

Wesley, John. "On the Use of Money." In *Sermons on Several Occasions*, vol. 4. Leeds: T.H. Hannon, 1799.

Wilkinson, Alan. *Christian Socialism: Scott Holland to Tony Blair*. London: SCM Press, 1988.

Wilkinson, Richard, and Kate Pickett. *The Spirit Level: Why Equality Is Better for Everyone*. London: Penguin, 2009.

Williams, Rowan. "Face It: Marx Was Partly Right about Capitalism." *The Spectator*, 26 September 2008.

———. "Knowing Our Limits." In *Crisis and Recovery: Ethics, Economics and Justice*, edited by Rowan Williams and Larry Elliott. Basingstoke: Palgrave Macmillan, 2010.

Wink, Walter. *Engaging the Powers*. Minneapolis: Fortress, 1992.

———. *Naming the Powers*. Minneapolis: Fortress, 1984.

———. *The Powers That Be*. New York: Doubleday, 1998.

———. *Unmasking the Powers*. Minneapolis: Fortress, 1986.

Wood, Diana. *Medieval Economic Thought*. Cambridge: Cambridge University Press, 2002.

Zarlenga, Stephen A. *The Lost Science of Money*. Valatie, NY: American Monetary Institute, 2002.

Lightning Source UK Ltd.
Milton Keynes UK
UKHW02f0629170118
316275UK00018B/569/P